THE LIFE OF
KING DAVID

*How God Works Through
Ordinary Outcasts and
Extraordinary Sinners*

J.S. Park

Copyright © 2015 by J.S. Park
Publisher: The Way Everlasting Ministry
Published August 2015, Edited March 2016

Cover art by Rob Connelly. http://heyitsrob.com

Scripture quotations are from the Holy Bible, New International Version®, NIV®.
Copyright © 1973, 1978, 1984, by International Bible Society. All rights reserved.
All quoted Scripture is from the New International Version 1984, and is also God-breathed and useful for teaching, rebuking, correcting, and training in righteousness.

Citation Information:
J.S. Park, *The Life of King David* (FL: The Way Everlasting Ministry, 2015) p. __

Park, J.S., author.
    The life of king David: how God works through ordinary outcasts and extraordinary sinners /
J.S. Park.—First edition.
    Includes bibliographical references.

ISBN 978-0692472637
    1. Old Testament—Religious—Christianity 2. Christian Life—Spiritual Growth
    3. Christian Life—Devotional

Printed in the United States of America.
10 9 8 7 6 5 4 3 2 1

Also the author of:
What The Church Won't Talk About
Mad About God
Cutting It Off

Join me in the journey of faith.

Wordpress. http://jsparkblog.com
Facebook. http://facebook.com/pastorjspark
Tumblr. http://jspark3000.tumblr.com
Podcast. http://thewayeverlasting.libsyn.com
Twitter. http://twitter.com/pastorjs3000
YouTube. http://youtube.com/user/jsparkblog

DEDICATED

For Pastor Jake English,
who was one of the very first pastors I knew
to bring the Bible to life.

For Pastor Paul Kim,
who made the Christian life make sense.

THE ROYAL TABLE
OF CONTENTS

PREFACE:
DAVID, OVER COFFEE

Some years ago, I preached a seven part sermon series on the life of King David, and it remains the most downloaded series on my podcast (except, of course, for sermons about sex and dating). People love David. His life has captivated us throughout history, a sweeping multi-layered drama of a simple man in extraordinary circumstances. Even the phrase "David and Goliath" is a faithful staple of our culture, regardless of belief or era. He's the epitome of rags to riches, the underdog who wins. Then there's the vulnerable, desperate side of David — his awful, embarrassing affair with a married woman and the subsequent murder of her husband. But no one ever takes it too hard on David. It's probably because he's not much different than us. We see ourselves in him.

There's just something about David. He's a mirror for the world; he's a reflection of every human heart. He's not only one of the most important people who ever lived, but a man I would love to talk with over coffee, to understand the pulse of the universe.

I've read his story many, many times. I often yell at David like he was a clueless character in a horror movie, bewildered that he provokes such ruin which could easily be avoided. But over time, I've realized I've felt the same way about myself. As the inimitable C.S Lewis has said, we're quite good at resenting others while excusing ourselves for the very same behaviors. Or as he puts it, "In our own case we accept excuses too easily; in other people's we do not accept them easily enough[1] ... We must love [the other person] more; and we must learn to see ourselves as a person of exactly the same kind."[2]

What I hated in David is what was destroying me, too.

What I loved in David is what I wanted to become.

David had a profound understanding of the weight of his own sin, yet he also comprehended the unrelenting love of his Creator. David was small before a holy, fearsome, unbearably perfect God, yet David rose confidently from shame by God's unbelievable grace. And so we are: deeply flawed, yet still beloved, by a God both ferocious and forgiving.

The first four chapters of this book are about God working through David the nobody, and the last three chapters are about redeeming David the sinner. In reading about David, we find not only the depth of our own vices and value, but the God who is at the center of this drama, beckoning us home to be the people we were meant to be. In David, we also find a universal, unanswered longing, dripping with the first foreshadows of a savior who was yet to come.

This is David's story. It is the story of a no-one who didn't matter, but became someone by knowing the Only One who does. It is our story.

---

[1] C.S. Lewis, *The Weight of Glory* (NY: HarperCollins, 1949, 1980) p. 181
[2] C.S. Lewis, *God in the Dock* (MI: Eerdmans, 1970) p. 154

AUTHOR'S NOTE

For the best reading on David's life, I recommend going straight to the source: the books of 1st and 2nd Samuel, much of the Psalms, and a bit of 1st Kings and 1st Chronicles. I would love for you to open it up as we travel together. The following work is a "literary dynamic devotional," which entails personal insight from multiple readings of the biblical text, grounded over a framework of Christ-centric hermeneutics, a seminary degree (that has kept me warm many a night), and cold hard experience. It incorporates theology, philosophy, psychology, application, and the genre of narrative, all which are meant to bridge the world of David's faith to your own faith journey. The book necessarily contains some creative riffing and a bit of theological speculation, and I try my best to indicate where the text ends and where my thoughts begin.

As the human brain is three lbs. and alarmingly squishy, I'm prone to some imaginative digressions that you may feel free to enjoy, abhor, or expand upon as the Spirit so illuminates. Alas, I am one person, and I must confess that I do not get it right all the time, and I hope we will still be friends where our interpretations may disagree and differ. As with any extra-biblical work on Scripture, I encourage a healthy lens of discernment and investigation, and I beg of your grace as we travel through the riches of God's Word.

—J.S.

PART 1

STONE SLINGER THE BOY KING

CHAPTER 1
EVERYTHING GREAT IN YOU
IS GOD IN YOU

Man looks at the outward appearance,
but the LORD looks at the heart.

1 Samuel 16

An Existential Price Check:
Giving Yourself a Grade

When we first meet David, he's really a nobody.

He's toiling away behind the scenes, a lonely kid in a field, completely ignored and unrecognized, with no hint that he'd one day be a king.

In the eyes of the few who knew him, including himself, he was practically worthless. If I could time-travel three-thousand years ago to interview David and ask him, "How much do you think you're worth?" — he might have shrugged and said, "Not very much. I just throw rocks from my sling all day. I write songs called psalms and I'm in charge of my dad's stubborn sheep. Sometimes I guard them from lions and bears. But none of that will ever pay off. Also, cool time machine."

If I were to ask you, "How much do you think you're worth?"

—

How would you answer?

If you were to measure your own worth on a number scale of 1 to 100 — What would that number be? How would you grade yourself?

Try it with me. *How much am I worth?* It's a bit harder than you think.

We'd have to start with a metric. We could estimate our usefulness to society and cultural prosperity and what talents and resources we bring to our city. We could ask how beneficial we are to our immediate friends and family. We could measure in our looks and smarts and wealth and charity. And God forbid, we could even measure our value by seeing the aftermath of our lives cut short.

How much am I really worth?

It sounds like a silly question, but we subconsciously ask it all the time. And we size up other people the same way we size up ourselves.

Everyone secretly has a **Point Value System**. It's often based on what we bring to the table. It's built on what we look like to the world.

How much am I really worth?

When I've asked this question in a group, most people are too modest to give a high number. I once asked some college students in a Bible study, "Write down five good traits about yourself and five bad ones." Everyone could do five bad ones. Most of them had trouble coming up with even two or three good ones. A lady in the group wrote a dozen bad traits about herself. She started crying because she couldn't think of a single good trait. The group rushed in, but the damage was done. I felt terrible about the whole thing and never did it again.

I did learn something. Those students in the Bible study confronted our tricky dilemma: that we need to be told there's good in us because we so often feel worthless, but we need to be worth something without being arrogant or needy. We're on a razor-thin edge of a pendulum between such unstable extremes.

I learned that it's horrifying to think we have a low value. It's also intoxicating to think we have a high value. Whether you think so or not: ***Everybody wants to be somebody.*** You want to be worth something. No one wants to be worth nothing.

You won't hear many people say, "I want to be somebody" out loud, but there was a bald honesty about that group of students that doesn't always show up everywhere else: that when we think about it hard enough, our own self-worth is always circling a low number because we each have an innate apprehension of our own inadequacy, and we each need to find our "value" by what we do and how we're seen.

There's a sense that we fall short of some kind of goodness and the universe will catch up and expose us somehow, and it's a constant looking over-the-shoulder that drags at our heels with *Or-Else*. I don't mean to stir up false discontent or anything. I think you already know what I mean. It's as if we're always leaking and trying to put the blood back in the wound, and we settle for shadows of beauty to patch it up, but it only holds together so long. A make-over can only make me so attractive; money can only make me so safe; these trophies can only make me so good; but the whisper pulls at the back of my teeth: *It's not enough.* It's an endless audition.

In the long run, we must either puff ourselves up to ignore the insecurity inside, or we're crushed by our awful self-regard. The entire world's solution for your worth is to do more and have more, and to convince you that this is *who you are* and *how you should feel.*

I want you to know this is a lie. There's a better truth.

So let's start again. *How much are you really worth?*

And where did you get that number?

The Boy King:
The First Ignored and the Last in Line

THE DRAMATIS PERSONAE —

- Samuel the Prophet, tasked to find a king

- Jesse, the father of said prophesied king

- David, the youngest son of Jesse and unknown shepherd boy; not a king

The first time we read about David in the Book of First Samuel, he's not even in the scene. His family is told to grab him from the field, where he's been tending sheep, and no one wants to get him.

It's a special day. Jesse, the father of David, has been called with his sons to a kind of fairground parade, where the prophet Samuel is choosing the future King of the Israelites. It was a big deal. King Saul has been rejected as the king, and Samuel has gotten the divine message to anoint a new one. He would be the first official King of Israel.

The seven sons of Jesse have formed a line before Samuel. Of course, Eliab, the eldest son, thinks it has to be him. The eldest son traditionally had all the privilege, a cultural staple called primogeniture, and it was as good as law. Eliab probably has no doubt in his mind, *I'm totally the king*. Even the prophet Samuel is sure it must be him.

But Samuel hears from God:

"Do not consider his appearance or his height, for I have rejected him. The LORD does not look at the things people look at. People look at the outward appearance, but the LORD looks at the heart." (1 Samuel 16:7)

Eliab gets to the end of the catwalk, but Samuel turns him down. I'm sure the townspeople made a singular gasp. The original hearers of this story might have been confused and appalled. Is Samuel wrong? Does Eliab start over? Does Samuel request Eliab to walk a second, third, tenth time?

Jesse's second son Abinadab has to be thinking, *It's totally me*. He walks, but nothing. The third son Shammah walks, and nothing. When all seven sons have passed, Samuel asks, "Are these all the sons you have?"

They must've flinched at the same time.

Jesse says, perhaps with a sheepish grin, "There is still the youngest. He is tending the sheep." And the unsaid thoughts hanging in the air: *It can't be David. Not him.*

But Samuel has his orders. He's heard what he's heard.

The Lord doesn't look at the appearance. He looks at the heart.

Samuel the Prophet must've gotten irritated, because he immediately sends a messenger to the field and says, "No one sit down until he arrives."

They all must've flinched again. The youngest brother?

We cut to David, a boy in a beautiful green pasture under a marble blue sky, alone with his sheep: his only friends. I'm imagining a flute playing in the background, like *Lord of the Rings,* a yellow butterfly circling David's head. Except this is just another grueling day of work for David, a lot of standing around and sticky armpits and sweating under his robes. It was stinky, hot, and boring. The most exciting moment was when the sun began its crawl below the horizon. It sounds romantic to be a shepherd, unless you're actually there.

During this time, the job of a shepherd was the kind you settled for. It was dirty and degrading. David, the youngest of the family, was handed down this unceremonious task because the youngest of the children was considered the least valuable. It's also possible that David's father owed a debt, so he "volunteered" David for indentured servitude. David was a sold-out slave-boy, tucked away in a tiny unseen corner of the universe, hidden from the town, invisible to his family.

It must've been downright gut-wrenching when the messenger comes to David and tells him about the anointing. *Wait,* David probably thinks, *my dad left me behind?*

There could've been a moment when David considers staying with his sheep. He could've clenched his staff, grit his teeth, wiped his eyes, pounded his fists. He must have thought, *It won't be me anyway. I could never be a king. My dad doesn't even call me a son.*

This part of the story is painful because it's so personal. I've been there. I've been the first ignored and the last picked and the terribly unwanted. It's a burden to feel unattractive and unseen all the time. There's not much worse than being called a zero.

This might have been the end of the story for David. "No thanks," he could've told the messenger, voice shaking and hands tight. "Just tell them you couldn't find me." Or, "How dare they forget me? Tell them I'm done with this family."

I would've understood. Yet David goes, unhindered by rejection. He's not controlled by his family's opinion of him. He's not controlled by his own opinion of himself. David probably didn't know it, but it took him both a humility and a confidence to leave that field for the fairground. He was humble enough not to resent his family, but confident enough not to wallow in pity. He neither thought too much of himself nor too little. He's somehow both grounded and is two feet off the ground.

David didn't live inside such appearances. He lived in a deeper place, within a glorious heartbeat above a world addicted to the shadow of beauty.

How? Perhaps it's because David had plenty of solitude in the field, pondering his place in the world, wondering if he would amount to anything. I'm sure he grew up hearing the stories *Yahweh,* the always-loving, awe-inducing Creator, who had divinely imbued all His people with a purpose, a plan, and power. David must have known the story of the Exodus, where God rescued the enslaved Israelites by complete mercy, not demanding His people to do a single thing to be saved, but leading them out by His own will. Maybe one of David's favorite passages was Deuteronomy 7:7-8, which says,

"The LORD did not set his affection on you and choose you because you were more numerous than other peoples, for you were the fewest of all peoples. But it was because the LORD loved you and kept the oath he swore to your ancestors that he brought you out with a mighty hand and redeemed you from the land of slavery, from the power of Pharaoh king of Egypt."

God didn't rescue the Israelites because they were the biggest or best, when in fact, they were the smallest and the least. God simply chose to love the Israelites out of His own nature.

If you think of every claim of love, it's almost always contingent on something. "I love you — because of how you look, how you laugh, how you serve, how you write and speak and dance and sing and lead." No one says it this way, but we all fall in love with someone's traits and usefulness and potential. Yet those things will eventually die out because we're turning to dust, one day at a time. Under an X-ray, we're all skeletons. If you fixate your love for someone on any single reason, that reason will get worn and withered.

God's sort of love isn't like that. It's not like human love. It has no reason to exist except that it does. *I love you because I love you.* God's love is eternally grounded *in* Himself and *for* you. His love is not a matter of your maintenance, but awakening, that you'd simply believe His love to be there and true.

Despite David's situation, he would know his worth was not grounded in his career, his birth right, or his family's casual dismissal. On some basic, child-like level, David grasped a love that did not count him against himself. *David knew a love not based in external value, but an intrinsic worth in The One who made him.*

We can put it this way. In 1998, Mark McGwire hit a record-breaking seventieth home run, and the next year, the home run ball sold at an auction for *three million dollars.* A baseball usually costs about five bucks — but because of *who* the baseball was associated with, it exponentially increased the value. We see this sort of thing all the time. If Elvis Presley or Marilyn Monroe or Bruce Lee previously owned an everyday item, others will pay big money for it because of the owner. *The owner ascribes worth to the item.* The item is worth nothing. The owner is worth everything.

You and I need something outside of us to give us worth. If you don't believe me, we only need to look around. Walk into a crowded room and watch for a little while: everyone's scrambling to grab the same bag of points, trying to top each other's story, scratching for glory, landing the right jokes, proving they belong. Every group is a high school reunion.

David was permanently stamped with a low ceiling of worth from his family, because this was the value system of his ancient Eastern world; all he could ever amount to was a shepherd and a youngest son. This sounds archaic and regressive, but we're no different. Our modern Western world defines value by the values we defy. An independent, individualistic, dream-chasing student will defy their parents' religion or a magazine's body-image or a certain political party, and then find a cheering section in social media and clearly drawn camps of tribalistic, self-congratulatory views. It's exchanging one choir for another. It's hijacking worth to be worthy, and it swells us by snobbery. It also divides. The rich sneer at the poor, the poor despise the rich, the famous feel more relevant, the unknown harbor resentment. And the second you and I fail those choirs: we're destroyed by the gate-keepers. It's just as restrictive. Even humility, as Apostle Paul says, can be a form of bragging.[3]

You find your worth somewhere: but the problem is that you'll eventually fail the ones who hold your worth, and you'll be crushed or abandoned. Or you'll be the one who stomps on others and leaves them behind.

It's not enough to tell yourself that you're good.

It's not enough to be told that you're good.

---

[3] Colossians 2:18, 23

You need someone who's truly good to call you good, even in your nothingness and failure.

God anointed David, not because David was extraordinary, but because God is incredibly extravagant, and *only the Creator can ascribe true worth to His creation.* Not people and not our points, but simply God Himself. David never had to prove his worth, but simply received his worth from the only One who was worthy. He didn't need outside beauty. He had the real thing.

Young David only had to show up. He enters the fairgrounds and Samuel the Prophet anoints him on the spot. We're told *"from that day on the Spirit of the LORD came powerfully upon David."* David had years to ascend the throne, but from that day on, God was going to pour through a raggedy, rugged shepherd to do God's greatest.

Everything that was great in David was the greatness of God. Everything that's great in you will always be God in you, because the irreducible fingerprint of God is your bottom-most foundation, and it is irrevocable. You can rest in that. You have a worth apart from what you do or what you have, simply because God has breathed you into existence. If you're breathing, you matter, because you matter to the One who gave you breath.

"Are not five sparrows sold for two pennies? Yet not one of them is forgotten by God. Indeed, the very hairs of your head are all numbered. Don't be afraid; you are worth more than many sparrows."

— Luke 12:6-7

A Psychological Ploy:
"I'm Just Fine Without God."

When I tell someone, "Everything great in you is God in you," the objection I often hear is, "Isn't this what Christians are supposed to say? Isn't it a psychological ploy to help Christians feel special? What about those rich, famous, successful people who never needed God? Aren't they doing great, too? Can't we do great things apart from God?"

It's true: I believe we can do some wonderful things apart from a belief in God. And maybe "God's love" is just a mental thumbs-up to keep you warm for a little while. I only offer the following thought for consideration.

In Matthew 6, when Jesus is preaching the famous Sermon on the Mount, he talks about those who give, fast, and pray in public. They're showing off. Jesus makes the startling statement, *"Truly I tell you, they have received their reward in full."*

What's he saying? Jesus is remarking that those who puff up their good deeds are rewarding themselves with their own praises. Our default mode is to focus on ourselves, because the initial ego-boost feels so good. It's doing good to look good and to get good back — which diminishes any good we could possibly do. It becomes less about the thing we're doing and more about ourselves.

In my first year of preaching as a pastor, I was obsessively neurotic about being winsome and engaging. My sermons always had a second language underneath: "Aren't I good? Isn't this funny? Won't you like me?" I brought in shocking punch-lines and the saddest tragedies and tons of alarming statistics to rouse the crowd. If they laughed or cried or took notes or nodded, I felt alive. It was flesh-driven and fishing for approval.

It was also disastrous. One of the problems was my mood fluctuated from sermon to sermon. If I preached a good one, I had an amazing week. If I bombed, I was miserable trying to improve for next week. I might preach ten good sermons in a row, but it felt like I was crawling on thin ice, constantly anxious I would fail. The other problem was that such a fragile motive never bore fruit. Sermons are supposed to be a way of loving people, but really, I was only loving myself. People caught on. There was no heart, no spirit, no serving, just slick calculation — and such things never last. Fluffy sermons and long-distance charity and click-bait blogs are flashy spurts of glamour, but they have no staying power.

The motives of those who do great things in their own power is often for the sake of their own greatness, and *a greatness started in the self will end in itself because it seeks nothing else but itself.*

Our motives matter. It turns us into a certain kind of people. Someone who hogs all the credit and glory only becomes more arrogant and small. Someone who keeps missing it becomes crippled by their failures. Every victory is vanity and every loss is soul-crushing despair. We either brag or break down. We end up dancing on a slippery stage of praise and punishment.

Jesus in Matthew 6 is implying: If you could be secure in who you were before you did a single thing, then you could do the actual thing without using it to validate you. When I say, "Every-thing great in you is God in you," it means *you have the praise of the praiseworthy.* It's the only praise big enough to fill you so that you won't have to hijack it from anywhere else. You can rest. It's a done deal. If God has already ascribed your worth, you're free to do good things out of their own goodness instead of chasing them to make you good. When your motive is no longer to "be good" but to look to the only One who *is* good, you can quit looking to the world to make you strong, but instead move in the strength you already have. You'd be free from the Desperate Race of Validation. That means truly living from the heart: a heart fully filled.

When we read about David's brothers prancing in front of Samuel the Prophet, it's easy to laugh at them. I'm sure they were strutting as proudly as possible. I would've gotten a kick out of seeing them booted off stage. But I'm no better than them. My ego always wants more ego. I'm the king of my own tiny empire. It's a shaky little stage where I strut all day, until either it collaps-es or I do.

I think David was chosen because he didn't want to be the king. He thought he was a nobody. And that's the sort of person God is looking for: someone who isn't singing his own praises. He doesn't care about big stages. It's only this sort of person that leverages his throne to serve others without making it about himself.

I'm reminded of Harry Potter and the Sorcerer's Stone. The evil Lord Voldemort is looking for the stone to create a potion of immortality, but Harry Potter only wants the stone to keep it safe. It turns out that the stone will go to the person who wants it most but who wants to use it least — in other words, to a person of good intentions who won't abuse the power they're given. The Sorcerer's Stone, one of the most powerful objects in the series, is given to the least powerful child.

God looked into the heart of David and saw a boy who was neither attached nor corrupted by the lie of appearances. He would not rise and fall on the tide of opinion and prestige and self-assigned points. He truly lived from his heart.

God looks for those who know they're nothing so that He can do something. If we already think we're something, then we've received our reward in full, because we are, in fact, full of ourselves. God *wants* to do something through us, but He will not force His own way into someone whose cup is already filled with himself. It starts with knowing we're nobodies.

It's not easy. It requires a heart-ripping humility that most of us can't bear. It requires knowing that every good thing we do comes from the Very Greatest.

The truth is that objectively speaking, David was a nobody. His family, in a sense, was right. He was simply dust of the earth. But so too were his family and the prophets and the kings, and so too are we. We're all worth "zero" when we stand before a holy, perfect God. But it's this very same God who does away with counting at all. As C.S. Lewis puts it so well:

"The infinite value of each human soul is not a Christian doctrine. God did not die for man because of some value He perceived in him. The value of each

human soul considered simply in itself, out of relation to God, is zero. As St. Paul writes, to have died for valuable men would have been not divine but merely heroic; but God died for sinners. He loved us not because we were lovable, but because He is Love" [4]

Only a person who knew they were both a zero and infinity could be radically grateful and recklessly secure. It's the only way we'd be knocked out of our selfish orbits, towards each other, to have an other-centered life that cares less about what we get for ourselves. It wouldn't be about you or me anymore, but about the God and people we're serving and the God who allows us to serve them.

This is why God crowned the unlikeliest kid in town. If a boy can be called a king before he does a single worthy thing, he would know where he came from and where he's headed. He would never, ever have to question his place in such a kingdom of certainty. And he could serve just to serve, a nobody serving nobodies.

That's you. That's me. A nobody made into somebody by the only One who can make us someone.

"God made the world out of nothing, and as long as we are nothing, He can make something out of us."

— Martin Luther

[4] C.S. Lewis, *The Weight of Glory* (NY: HarperCollins, 1949, 1980) p. 146

The Impossible Love for the Unlovable

I always cheer when I read about David's anointing. Not because I have anything against his brothers. Not because of wish-fulfillment for revenge-by-success. But because I have hope for guys like me. It's the same hope for you, too. A hope for those who have been left out, shoved to the back, and seen as second-class.

Years ago, I watched a daytime talk show hosted by Ricki Lake. It was one of those tacky, unsettling talk shows that leaves you feeling sad about the human race. This particular episode, men and women who were "unattractive" as children had gotten plastic surgery, gone to the gym, gotten rich, and were now completely made over. They each met a person from their past on the show, like a bully or a former crush. One of the made-over women, who had changed a lot since her high school photo, faced off a guy who had mercilessly picked on her all throughout high school. When the guy came out, the woman did a dance around the guy and the crowd cheered. She demanded an apology. The guy countered, "You still look like the same ugly kid. You're still ugly in your face."

The crowd was horrified. Ricki Lake flinched. But most of all, the woman was devastated. The show quickly cut to a commercial break.

Even though I was not a Christian while watching the show, I kept thinking to myself, *Can't people just be loved without the make-*

over? Do these people really need to show off how much they've changed? Do we have to put so much stock in how we look?

I kept thinking about that woman, and all the effort she invested, only to be told, "You're still ugly in your face." No amount of surgery or make-up or exercise was going to compensate for the hole inside.

I really hurt for her, and for me.

I wish I could have told her she was treasured, prized, and loved, apart from what she looked like and what other people had said to her.

I wish I could say with confidence that I was loved, too, but I was just as fractured as the woman and just as destructive as the bully.

I think even then, before I knew God, I knew what we were looking for —

For a love that knows us exactly as we are, who sees even our innermost ugliness, and still calls us beloved. Such a love is the wholeness we need.

Isn't that we want? Someone who knows us, yet loves us anyway?

Years later, I found that such an impossible love exists.

Our True King:
Humbled, Humiliated, and Glorious

"How glorious the splendor of a human heart which trusts that it is loved!" [5]

— Brennan Manning

In Luke 24, Jesus tells us that the entire Old Testament was talking about himself. We discover that David was the predecessor for a Greater David, who became the True King of a new kingdom — but not a king or kingdom like we have ever seen before.

In the Kingdom of God — by which I mean, in the purview of God's activity and wisdom — there is a total reversal of values. Those who want to be first must be last[6]; those who are humble will be exalted[7]; those who lose their life will save it[8]; the meek will inherit the earth;[9] and the least among us is the greatest.[10]

While David was a servant who became a king, Jesus was a king who became a servant, who left his heavenly throne to walk in the dirt and grit of his people. We learn that Jesus, the very Son of God, was born in humility, in an out-of-town manger to teenage parents of a nobody town called Nazareth, and like

[5] Brennan Manning, *Ruthless Trust* (NY: HarperCollins, 2000) p. 148
[6] Matthew 20:16
[7] Matthew 23:12, Luke 14:11, 1 Peter 5:6, James 4:6, Proverbs 3:34
[8] Matthew 10:39, 16:25, Mark 8:35, Luke 9:24, 17:33
[9] Matthew 5:5, Psalm 37:11
[10] Matthew 19:30, Luke 9:48

David, was rejected in his own hometown. But Jesus, the True King, didn't build from the brightest. He recruited the meek, the poor, and the persecuted: the people who were last in their field. He called the not-good-enough, the lost cause, the raggedy, despicable, beat-down, busted up sinner. He called people like you and me. He picked the pimps and politicians and aristocrats and lepers and blind beggars, those on the very fringes who were considered worthless in the eyes of a shaming world. With these, Jesus made his upside-down kingdom.

Jesus evened the playing field. He subverted the point-system. He left out no one. All of Scripture tells us that we don't need to fight for the inner-circle anymore. We're told we don't have to claw for a throne, for the throne came to us.

What I love about God is that He picks weird, awkward, empty, frail vessels like you and me to flex his crazy, glorious Kingdom. No one else does this but Him.

But Jesus went one further. He didn't automatically pick the outcast, but it's that the outcast knew what the successful did not: that we all have such sin that makes us truly unworthy. The sick know they need a doctor,[11] and we all carry the sickness of sin. Jesus loved the sinner anyway. He traversed the ugliness of our sinful hearts and bore the hostility of a hateful world. It cost Jesus his life. It's only an endlessly costly love that's worth enough to purchase us from sin and make us new as gold. Jesus not only had to catch the rejection of those who rejected us,

---

[11] Matthew 9:12, Mark 2:17, Luke 5:31

but endured our own rejection, too. He "made himself nothing," even going to a cross, naked and humiliated, sharing in
our worst pain, made ugly and horrific to the human eye, [12] and
was stripped of all his worth to give it over to us. He jumped
out of a grave to find us and bestow on us his righteousness.
He had the absolute power as a king to crush us, but he instead
used it to become one of us, and to love us.

He loves you for no other reason except that He does, out of
His very own being. When we're pierced by this kind of one-way,
self-initiated love, we're re-made by such selfless love, revoked of
every pretense, motivated by the motive of no-motive. From the
heart.

If we encounter the infinitely powerful God, we find we are
truly nothing; yet when we encounter the surprisingly humble
God, we find we are truly glorious. There would be no use for
high self-esteem or low self-esteem, because we would have no
esteem. We would be humble enough to quit affixing points on
others, but confident enough to quit subtracting points from
ourselves. We have nothing and everything, at the same time. We
are zero plus infinity.

The Christian is no longer tethered to results or recognition.
When you remove the umbilical cord of self-validation and plug
into the cosmic constancy of God, you'll taste a reckless freedom
and joy in all you do. You quit getting nervous on the other end.
A good turn-out is a bonus and not a verdict. Talent is not the

[12] Philippians 2:7, Isaiah 52:14

ceiling on success. Your past is not a time-stamp of the world's critical eye. The God-given capacity to serve is its own reward. It isn't for applause, but out of gratitude. And your excellence is not crafted for praise, but for its very own existence: just as God loves you, simply for existing.

Can you imagine? You wouldn't care how you look, what you lose, or what you can and can't do. Such a person is fearless. You'd simply be you.

At the feet of True Greatness, you find a humble strength to become who you always knew you could be.

"Imagine how a man's life would be if he trusted that he was loved by God. How he could interact with the poor and not show partiality, he could love his wife easily and not expect her to redeem him, he would be slow to anger because redemption was no longer at stake, he could be wise and giving with his money because money no longer represented points, he could give up on formulaic religion, knowing that checking stuff off a spiritual to-do list was a worthless pursuit, he would have confidence and the ability to laugh at himself, and he could love people without expecting anything in return. It would be quite beautiful, really." [13]

— Donald Miller

---

[13] Donald Miller, *Searching For God Knows What* (TN: Thomas Nelson, 2004, 2010) p. 177

A Word For You:
God Is Sowing

Right now, you could be toiling away unseen and unnoticed, waiting for your big break. You might be discouraged because nothing is paying off, or you feel you're constantly catching up to a version of someone you've yet to be. You could be compensating for a failure behind you or trying to prove your merit to the people around you.

No one likes this part, because we see everyone else's highlights and we presume they've got it together and we're relegated to second-rate status. We might even feel that our current work is beneath our true potential. We want to be doing "great things," but we're stuck in limbo, in that icky middle.

The truth is that you can prosper right where you are. You can still be teachable in your season behind-the-scenes, even if that season is for life. God's greatness is available to you so long as you remain available. No one needs to climb the throne to get there. I believe even rejected guys like Saul and Eliab were still redeemable, because it doesn't take a king to do good work. You only need to be present and presently engaged.

This is tough, because we're so used to climbing the pecking order. We're tempted to superimpose a future hologram of big stages and big audiences on our current station. But such fantasies draw us out of engagement with *now*. There's work to be done today, no matter the size of your stage. Your effort doesn't always have to "pay off." Some of us want to be the king of our fields overnight, but God has already called His children a royal priesthood,[14] and we're called to harvest for a lifetime.[15] No matter what kind of work you're doing, it's essential in the tapestry of God's Kingdom.

The lie is that "doing great things for God" must look huge like Hollywood. It's possible that you're called to China or to Uganda or to sell all your stuff for charity. That would be awesome. But great things also include: raising your kids, writing a song, greeting on Sundays, listening over coffee, and loving your next-door neighbor. Also awesome. If you're teaching five people at a Bible study, if you have twenty followers on your blog, if your church hasn't grown past fifty — you're still a vehicle for God to flex His power as a force for good in the universe. God is still in the business of using rejected, empty, unknown people for His glorious story on the earth.

God is sowing. He is sovereign. He is doing His wildly wonderful work in you, not by the flip of a switch, but by the journey of a seed pushing through the dirt into the warmth of the sun.

So serve that tiny place. Be okay in the background. Work hard in the field.

We need the unsung heroes.

We need you.

---

[14] 1 Peter 2:9
[15] Galatians 6:9

CHAPTER 2
HOW THE WEAPON OF GRACE CONQUERED GOLIATH

David triumphed over the Philistine
with a sling and a stone.

1 Samuel 17

The Best Winners Are the Losers

Everyone loves an Underdog Story.

Whether it's Rocky, Annie, Harry Potter, John McClane, or Jackie Chan — we root for the underdog. The bigger and badder the villain, the better their fall. The pluckier the hero, the more satisfying their victory.

The story of David and Goliath strikes an inherent chord in all of us. It's perhaps the most well known Bible story in popular culture. When a lone lawyer takes down an evil corporation, the news says "David takes down Goliath." I'm a sucker for the Hero Against-All-Odds, fighting the syndicate and exposing the corruption and dismantling the conspiracy. This sort of heroism taps into a shared, secret longing of every culture and narrative. Why?

I believe that because we're created in the image of God, the *imago Dei,*[16] we inherently know that "human strength" is wrong. There's a sense that overpowering another person or dominating someone's will is a terribly inhuman injustice, so we cheer on the Little Guy. We hate it when the cocky, smarmy bad guy wins. We wait for the montage when the hero trains to music and uses their scrappy ingenuity for a close-call finish.

If you ever want to write an award-winning Hollywood script, set your hero at a disadvantage and don't let them have it easy. You can do what *Guardians of the Galaxy* did: When the good guy announces his name, have the bad guy say, "Who?" Everyone can get behind that kind of guy.

The story of David versus Goliath is often preached as "facing your giants." I've heard Goliath compared to debt or a dead marriage or a dying business. The stones are supposed to be right habits or time management or Five Strategies For A Can't-Miss Career. Those might be fine sermons, but I don't think David would've told it that way. It's so much bigger than that. In fact, preaching Goliath as the "obstacle" in your way of success can be drastically harmful, because the message is the very opposite. The story of David the underdog isn't like any other story of the little guy winning.

As we go through the seventeenth chapter of First Samuel, you'll notice two opposing themes: the **Weapons of the World** and the **Weapons of the Kingdom of God**. And it's not merely

---

[16] Genesis 1:27

Violence versus Non-Violence, as David had to stand his ground — but something much deeper.

The Battle Before the Battle:
The Real Fight Is with Yourself

THE DRAMATIS PERSONAE —

- King Saul, the current king of Israel

- Goliath, the number one soldier of the Philistine army

- David, the young boy prophesied to be the next king

- Eliab, David's oldest brother

David has now become a food runner for the Israelite army, and his three oldest brothers have joined a brewing war against the Philistines. David runs food to the soldiers each day and runs back to tend his sheep. He's still doing grunt work, not a soldier, and certainly not a king.

As the war heightens to a face-off, Jesse the father of David commissions a food run directly to David's brothers. David brings roasted grain, ten loaves of bread, and ten blocks of cheese. Jesse also requests to ask how his sons are doing. The amount of food plus Jesse's request implies that it's not going well for the Israelites.

When David arrives on the scene, we find out why.

A ridiculously huge Philistine named Goliath, an experienced soldier almost ten feet tall, has been mocking the Israelite army for forty days. He's declared representative warfare by proxy: send out a single soldier from each side, and the winner takes all. This is good news and bad news. The good news is that it could save a lot of lives; the bad news is that Goliath's hand could probably crush a human head like a grape.

King Saul and his people have been running "dismayed and terrified" (verses 11 and 24). The Hebrew word terrified is sometimes the same word used for the "fear of the Lord," so Saul and the soldiers were literally treating Goliath as a god.

David arrives just as Goliath begins his taunt for the day, and David is mortified. Not scared, not shaken, but upset about everyone else's fear. David asks the nearby soldiers, "Who is this uncircumcised Philistine that he should defy the armies of the living God?" In other words, *If God is for us, who can be against us?*

David's oldest brother Eliab sees him and "burned with anger" (V. 28). Eliab gets really nasty with his brother, probably because he's still bitter about being turned down as the king. Eliab says to David, "Why have you come down here? And with whom did you leave those few sheep in the desert? I know how conceited you are and how wicked your heart is; you came down only to watch the battle."

This is an emasculating cheap shot. If I were David right then, I might do what any hot-blooded younger sibling would do: throw a punch and run.

But I absolutely love what David does instead. Verses 29 and 30 say,

"Now what have I done?" said David. "Can't I even speak?" **He then turned away** *to someone else and brought up the same matter, and the men answered him as before.*

In most conflicts, it's easier to retaliate. David had just been called a lying, selfish, evil, voyeuristic sheep-slave. But David counters in an almost philosophical way: *Is this really about me? Aren't I human? Aren't we here together?* And perhaps subliminally, *Why would you say that?*

I've actually tried this before. When I used to work as a cashier and a waiter, occasionally I was met with over-the-top racism. So I would pause and ask, "Why? Why would you say that?" It caught people off guard, and most of them flushed and apologized. If instead I tried to fight back, it only escalated out of control.

David then *turns away* from Eliab, to find out what was really happening. Again, if it were me, this would've gone very differently: I might have entangled myself in a squabble with my brother. But there was something much larger at stake than sibling rivalry. David addresses the distraction, and then regains his focus. He's on a mission. David doesn't get caught up in a petty drama; he re-affirms his right to be there, and then moves on to the urgent priority at hand.

I'm reminded of Colossians 3:2, in which Paul says,

Set your mind on things above, not on earthly things.

David finds King Saul and tells him, *"Let no one lose heart on ac-count of this Philistine; your servant will go and fight him"* (V. 32).

Saul tells David that he's just a boy. Goliath is a trained warri-or who happens to be as tall as two men. David suddenly re-members that as a shepherd, he protected his sheep from lions and bears. *"I went after it, struck it and rescued the sheep from its mouth. When it turned on me, I seized it by its hair, struck it and killed it."* (V.35)

This part has always made me laugh. I imagine a bear jumps through my window, and then a youth group student grabs the bear by his fur and face-punches him. One punch, and the bear's eyes roll up and he keels over with a roar. I'm not into hunting or anything, but if I saw a scrawny kid beat up a bear in his backyard, I would be very, very impressed.

David continues, *"Your servant has killed both the lion and the bear; this uncircumcised Philistine will be like one of them, because he has defied the armies of the living God. The LORD who delivered me from the paw of the lion and the paw of the bear will deliver me from the hand of this Philistine."* (V.36-37)

Maybe it's this story or maybe it's David's wide-eyed confi-dence, but King Saul agrees to the battle. I have to give Saul some credit here. He's now banking on this food-running, sheep-herding, harp-playing musician to represent the entire nation of Israel for its very future. I'm imagining if David had lost, Saul could've said, "Just kidding! That was a practice run."

King Saul gives over his armor, helmet, and sword to David, but David finds it so uncomfortable that he leaves them behind. I mean, really. I would've asked for at least a dagger.

This is a huge contrast to Goliath. Earlier in the passage, we're told that Goliath is wearing a bronze chest-plate weighing one-hundred twenty-five pounds and holding an iron spear that weighs fifteen pounds. He also has a servant carrying around his shield (which leads me to believe there are worse things than being a shepherd). If we include Goliath's bronze helmet and leg-pads, he's probably fitted with about two-hundred pounds of metal weaponry.

There's almost no other place in the Bible where such a description is given. Professor Robert Alter, a Jewish scholar and theologian, says that Goliath is "an almost grotesquely quantitative embodiment of a hero, and this hulking monument to an obtusely mechanical conception of what constitutes power is marked to be felled by a clever shepherd boy with his slingshot." [17]

David has a stick and a sling. He picks up five rocks from the river. And that's it. He doesn't even use the stick.

I'll Punch Your Other Cheek:
The City of Man and the Kingdom of God

I'd like to freeze-frame right here, so we can take it all in.

---

[17] Robert Alter, *The Art of Biblical Narrative* (NY: Basic Books, 2011) p. 103

In the exchange between David and his brother Eliab — David chooses to turn away instead of getting trapped in anger.

In the exchange between Goliath and King Saul — Saul runs and hides, terrified.

In the exchange between King Saul and David — David chooses to let go of the armor and sword, despite Goliath holding more weapons than David's entire weight.

These little contrasts exemplify an underlying truth from this passage: that the **Weapons of the World** are about reactionary violence and control, while the **Weapons of God's Kingdom** are about thoughtful action and patience.

Here's what I mean. When we see Goliath, he's dressed to kill and yelling for blood. He's about *Control.* The death-grip on control is a very popular Worldly Weapon. It manipulates people and things to feel power and to stay ahead in our Point Value System. When we see Saul, he's a shaking dot in the distance. He's about *Escape.* This is also another popular Worldly Weapon, and is simply the other side of the coin of control. If we can delay, avoid, blame, daydream, or run, then we never have to be responsible for anything.

If you look around, whether at the mall or on the news or at your church, you can see this happening right before your eyes. You'll know if someone is wielding Control by the little power-plays and pretend-shows of humility. You'll know the people who Escape when they bottle it all in and clutch onto resentment and future-fantasies.

You'll start to see this chasm between *Worldly* and *Divine* throughout Scripture, and of course, in life. Our immediate instinct is to go with our flesh. If you slapped me across the face, my hand would instantly form a fist to hit you back. But Jesus says, *"Turn the other cheek."* Paul in Roman 12 says, *"Do not repay anyone evil for evil ... Do not be overcome by evil, but overcome evil with good."* When David is mocked, he absorbs the offense and defuses the tension.

There's a kind of divine response that transcends our ordinary cycles of violence and disarms us by sheer surprise. I'm not surprised when I hear someone cheated on his spouse and left his kids or embezzled money from the fund or slandered me or punched that guy or cut her off or really hated me the whole time or totally sold out. But I'm surprised at forgiveness. I'm surprised when someone makes it right. I'm surprised when I hear, "I'm wrong" and "I'm sorry." Or "Here's what I owe." Or takes responsibility. Or defends someone behind their back. Or shakes my hand anyway.

Every once in a while, the heavens open and God breaks in and He interrupts our prickly, predictable ways.

The flesh is easy. The divine takes no less than divinity. This is the battle inside. We live smack-dab between the City of Man and the Kingdom of God. It's a tightrope. We fail at this every day, most especially me. We're each capable of retaliating in the flesh or responding from grace, and it's a daily decision to fight ourselves to fight for what matters.

Metal Dipped in Fire vs. Hands Dipped in a River:
The Sword Versus The Stone

There's another detail here that might help us. I've always been fascinated by David picking up *"five smooth stones from the stream."* In Scripture, almost nothing is described by physical appearance unless it has a narrative purpose. If someone is called smart or thrifty or beautiful, you can bet that person is gifted for a reason.

These "smooth" stones have been formed in the river for a long time, over a natural process of erosion by the current of the water. By comparison, Goliath's weapons and armor have been forged in the violent process of fire, smelting, hammers, and tempering.[18]

I'm probably reading too much into this, and analogies only go so far, but we're seeing a final contrast between David and Goliath. One has been formed by the quiet momentum of the elements, while the other has been molded by aggressive human hands. One was shaped by God's guidance of nature, while the other was twisted for coercion and destruction. When we contort things by our flesh, we forfeit God's power. In other words, no one will know God did anything. When you use brute strength, you leave no room for miracles.

The Philistines were also using brute force to win. If they had won: So what? They would've gone down in history as oppressive, barbaric bullies. Had David picked up the sword and

---

[18] I first heard this comparison from my friend John David Harris.

won, it would've been just as shallow. A worldly weapon can only bring a worldly victory.

My brother is a jujitsu champion and certified by the Gracie brothers. He owns a dojo and has trained Dave Batista. My brother is tall and skinny and he doesn't look like any MMA fighter you've seen. But he beats guys twice his size through pure skill. My brother used to say, "Skill will beat brute strength any day. And if the stronger guy wins, who cares? He just muscled his way in."

In fact, there's a lot of evidence that David was the better warrior. Malcolm Gladwell, a journalist, makes the case that David had superior weaponry, not burdened by bulky armor or bronze, and was armed with the equivalent of a handgun.[19] Goliath had brought a knife to a gun-fight. A slingshot required a wholly different accuracy than a sword. It was skillful. It was shaped by long hours of investment, to know where to strike.

We're going to approach people and problems in one of those two ways. We're either going after the outer-surface by slamming away, or we're getting to the inside by thoughtful, meticulous grace.

This doesn't mean we just play nice. This doesn't mean that you weaken your position. I'm not a pacifist or passive. We'll see that David does step into action. But we step into battle with a gentle spirit, with a steady resolve, with an almost aching humili-

---

[19] Malcolm Gladwell, *David and Goliath* (NY: Hachette, 2013) p. 11-12

ty. It will feel like losing, because it means letting go of our swords, our pride, our need to pay back. It requires the patience of a river polishing these jagged, rough edges, to permit smooth sailing.

It means what Jesus tells us in Matthew 10:16 — *"I am sending you out like sheep among wolves. Therefore be as shrewd as snakes and as innocent as doves."*

Clever like snakes; gentle like doves. A fine line, but that's how delicate it is.

Goliath was neither snake enough nor dove enough. He somehow both underestimated and over-compensated, which ended up sabotaging himself. David had a strategy to dismantle the danger, yet remained humble and true to who he was. He had both wits and character, both smarts and integrity. Like a stream, with focus and finesse.

This is exactly the balance it takes to lead, to grow, to change, and to see others change.

There's a kind of win that's really just losing. It's easy to strong-arm someone into submission so that they'd do what you say. It's a broad-sword approach. It pounds on the outside, but it never really internalizes. You can impose your point of view, shout over the table, and throw around your authority — but when you overpower enough people, you're left with no power and no people. You can attract people to your church with slick marketing or to your website with trashy ads — but you lose a little bit of yourself.

I've done all those things, and it always leaves me sick to my stomach and keenly aware that my "win" was never worth the cost. I try to force things to happen by an external apparatus of shaming or hype, and it might work for a little while, but it burns out just as fast. The irony is that by trying to win so hard, everyone loses.

The other way is harder. There's a slow kind of victory that emerges by actually caring and listening and learning, which takes a lot of time and attention. But everyone gets on board with such authenticity. Only a surgical grace with our full engagement ever goes deep enough to bring true change and unity.

It requires not getting offended too easily. It's being articulate and genuine and even charming without extra layers of glitz and gloss. It's hearing out everyone's story. It's long nights of being there. It's waiting instead of reacting. It's unclenching from perfectionism.

Paul in 2 Corinthians 10:3-4 says, *"For though we live in the world, we do not wage war as the world does. The weapons we fight with are not the weapons of the world. On the contrary, they have divine power to demolish strongholds."*

We're armed with patience and persistence, not bull-headed backlash.

Our best weapons are often empty hands and open arms.

But God chose the foolish things of the world to shame the wise; God chose the weak things of the world to shame the strong. He chose the lowly things of this world and the despised things—and the things that are not—to nullify the things that are, so that no one may boast before him.

— 1 Corinthians 1:27-29

The Showdown:
The Whole Dang Earth

Goliath laughs at this little kid on the battleground.

"Am I a dog that you come at me with sticks? Come here, and I'll give your flesh to the birds of the air and the beasts of the field!" I can hear the laughter, too, from both sides of the battle.

Right then, David gives a speech. He mentions God directly at least six times. He also takes Goliath's words and trumps them up to a whole other level. It's one of those moments that I'm sure is on replay in Heaven.

David says:

"You come against me with sword and spear and javelin, but I come against you in the name of the LORD Almighty, the God of the armies of Israel, whom you have defied. This day the LORD will hand you over to me, and I'll strike you down and cut off your head.

"Today I will give the carcasses of the Philistine army to the birds of the air and the beasts of the earth, and the whole world will know that there is a God in Israel. All those gathered here will know that it is not by sword or spear that

the LORD *saves; for the battle is the* LORD'S, *and he will give all of you into our hands."* (V.45-47)

I particularly like the thing with the birds and beasts. David takes everything that Goliath says and raises it one more notch. "Give my flesh to the birds, huh? I'll give them your *carcasses.* Give me over to beasts of the field? I'll give you over to beasts of the *whole dang earth.*"

I think Goliath must've been a little worried then, because he doesn't say another word. He walks into battle — and we see David *running.*

Here it is. A small shadow reaching across a great field, a boy whirling his sling in the air as it cuts a circle over his scrawny form, suddenly remembering those lonely days spent throwing rocks while tending dirty sheep, barely comprehending a glimpse of God's greater plan, the sun leaning across his back as the dust kicks up behind him, tiny footprints digging into where Goliath must have stood yelling each day, eyes squinting and face like a rock, the silence of soldiers watching intensely, the sound of history being made.

The stone is thrown.

It only takes one.

A shadow falls.

The earth shakes.

The air pulls in a gasp.

The boy has won.

The underdog has won.

Our True Victory:
The Ultimate Underdog

This story ends well for David: but I know it might not have for us.

Most of the time, the story of David and Goliath is preached as, "Be like David," but I think that's a little unfair. It's a discouraging moral parameter because many of us have thrown our rocks and missed. Or worse, we're more like Saul or Goliath. The truth is that not even David could be like David. We've all won the wrong battles or lost by trying too hard.

A thousand years after David killed Goliath, there was another man who stood up to the giant of sin, Satan, and death. He didn't take up rocks, but he took up a cross. There was a man who was a representative for all of us in the battlefield. The Greater David won the ultimate victory for us, but not by winning like the world does. He came to destroy all sin and all worldly weapons: by taking upon such darkness within himself. I hope we see the magnitude of such a thing. Jesus is the only person in history who has the right and power to retaliate; if not for all our injustice, then certainly for his innocence. I understand if he paid us back for the ways we've wronged him and wronged one another — but who's left standing in such a retributive cycle? It was in the cross that Jesus surprised us with grace. He could've retaliated, but he whispered forgiveness over the very people who were murdering him. It was there he cut our cycle of violence; he turned the other cheek and overcame evil with good; he suffered both with us and for us. He traded the worldly weapon of retribution for the divine weapon of forgiveness. He traded our sin, selfishness, and sorrow for joy, mercy, and eternal life. He won by losing in our place: yet he invites us to share in that victory.

In the cross, Jesus not only gave us grace but showed us the way of grace. The more we understand and embrace what Jesus did, the more it becomes unlikely, even impossible, to overpower others. Because when you know Jesus became weak out of humility and obeyed even to death on a cross, when you see that sort of love, it will re-create our hearts to be more like David, to be more like Jesus. Every time you want to act in the flesh, you only need to see what Jesus did for you instead.

When you also know that Jesus was a fellow underdog, who seemed defeated in death, then you'll find that failures are not the final word on you. The cross was not the last word on Jesus. The losses we incur on this earth can be awful, with little rhyme or reason, but there is a God who is with you in the battlefield, whose glory outshines all we will ever face. The resurrection is proof that we have already won. Our losses are only setbacks to where we're headed. If you're part of the story of Jesus: you have a good ending.

You might have failed to "be like David" today, but that's what Jesus came to do: to win on your behalf, so that you're not working *for* victory, but *from* it.

You're free to "lose" and fail and fall, because you don't have to win. The only battle that ever really matters has already been won for you by Jesus, who destroyed evil by rolling the stone.

That means even when the giants win sometimes, they're always standing in the shadow of a cross and a resurrection. *Goliath is not the real giant here, because even the most intimidating of men must live in the shadow of a glorious God.*

The title of "giant" belongs to only one.

"The gospel is the ultimate story that shows victory coming out of defeat, strength coming out of weakness, life coming out of death, rescue from abandonment. And because it is a true story, it gives us hope because we know that life is really like that.

"It can be your story as well. God made you to love Him supremely, but He lost you. He returned to get you back, but it took the cross to do it. He absorbed your darkness so that one day you can finally and dazzlingly become your true self and take your seat at His eternal feast." [20]

— Timothy Keller

---

[20] Timothy Keller, *King's Cross: The Story of the World in the Life of Jesus* (New York: Dutton, 2011) p. 230

A Word For You:
Getting Over the Underdog

Right now, you might be facing a ton of giants, and others have told you to "be the bigger person." This is good advice and I recommend it. Yet if everyone is trying to be the bigger person, we end up stomping on each other. If you treat every person and problem like Goliath, you'll be bitter all the time. It's a triumphalist, self-affirming theology that cries, "They're in my way." It stirs up a dichotomous conflict by turning people into obstacles and critics into haters. It keeps us in the cycle of retaliation.

Taking down Goliath means taking me down first. It's me. I'm the giant. I'm the bad guy.

The thing is, the idea of the "underdog" shouldn't even have to exist. It implies that there is "my side" versus "your side" and it forces me to demonize an opposition. We cheer when an underdog wins, but we forget that someone else had to lose. You might think you're the good guy, but to someone else, you're definitely the bad guy. So who is cheering for whom? Who gets to win?

Jesus is the only one who won every side by losing for them. In order to undo our back-and-forth, binary violence, Jesus stepped into the crossfire and called us all equally loved and heard, which meant that every side hated him for loving the other side. He got rid of sides. He crossed the dichotomous divide of demonization. The divide died on the cross with Jesus.

He called you a friend when you called him an enemy. Jesus killed his enemies by making them friends. And that's why they had to kill Jesus.

He's the only underdog who people rooted for to lose. That's how it had to work.

The story of David and Goliath ultimately shouts a counter-intuitive truth. It tells you to take off the gloves and lay down your metal and use the elements that God has shaped in the river of His patience.

The best weapon we can wield is grace.

The best war is love.

The best fight is forgiveness.

The best way is over coffee.

This is extremely difficult. It feels like getting stepped on. And maybe that's what grace will require sometimes.

Yet without such grace, we're only fighting a faceless target. We're yelling empty ideology. We turn real people into phantom enemies and cartoon villains. It's dehumanizing, and it's why we've destroyed each other since the very beginning. It is a feud without end.

You can end it.

When your family blows up into another argument at dinner — you can be the first to knock on every door, to apologize and tell them you love them.

When social media is acting up again with the same old hate and animosity — you can be the little bit of light and encouragement to remind others we're on the same team.

When everyone else is complaining and grumbling on the latest project and blasting the boss behind his back — you can speak life there, and work hard, and even love your boss.

When you're ready to call out the Pharisees and legalists and fundamentalists and "those kinds of Christians" — you can grieve for them instead, and keep your arms open.

I can't be against them. I'm them. You're them. And I'm crossing over, that grace might win.

Chapter 2.5
From Local Legend
To Hunted Fugitive

"Who am I ... that I should become the king's son-in-law?
... I'm only a poor man and little known. "

1 Samuel 18-20

The Irreversible, Unexpected Roller-Coaster of Life:
Staying on the Ground in the Ups-and-Downs

David becomes a rock-star overnight, and he plunges into a swirling spiral of fame, gossip, pop songs, envy, marriage, and murder, until he's running for his very life.

With the single throw of a stone: everything has changed.

You might have been there, too. We run into irreversible, unexpected turns in life, whether from success or failure, and the film of our lives has a clear splice of before-and-after. Many of us are unprepared for the changes. Some of us ride with the tide and compromise; others hate the new situation and never adjust. It's understandable. Both the spotlight and sudden loss have their own gravity, pulling us inexorably into a different kind of person. Some of us let these changes make us worse.

A few of us though, despite the whiplash, fight to retain that core inside. We don't forget where we came from. It doesn't mean we refuse to grow, but it does mean *we can still choose who we want to be.* When you firmly decide who you want to become, you won't let life throw you around into a version of someone you're not.[21]

I really like David in his early years of fame because he stays so rooted to that humble shepherd boy in the field. He turns down big rewards. He reaches out to the rejected. He stays grateful. He loves the haters. He never forgets who he is: an extravagantly blessed person who didn't earn or deserve a single thing he has. His wide-eyed simplicity often puts him at risk, but the one thing he never loses on the run is himself.

In four quick snap-shots, we see how David goes from local legend to hunted fugitive. In these snaps-shots, we see David's consistency of character.

1) They keep playing that same song. (1 Samuel 18)

David joins the army of Israel, and it turns out his battle with Goliath isn't a one-hit wonder. He starts winning battles left and right, and the Israelites start singing, *Saul has slain his thousands; David has slain his tens of thousands.* There's even a dance to it.

King Saul gets insanely jealous. I can understand. If someone used my name in a back-handed song to compliment someone else, it would bother me, too. "You're Bill Gates good, but not quite Steve Jobs good."

---

[21] We'll talk more about this in Chapters 4 and 5.

A sort of humorous cycle begins where King Saul sends David off to war to kill him, but David wins and becomes more popular. Saul offers his daughter Merab as a distraction, but David refuses: *"Who am I to become the king's son?"* Saul offers another daughter Michal, whom David actually likes, but he replies like before: *"Do you think it is a small matter to become the king's son-in-law? I'm only a poor man and little known."* This time Saul uses David's honor against him: "I'll let you have Michal for a hundred Philistine foreskins!" In other words, a hundred dead enemies for the king's daughter.

Saul is hoping that David will finally die in battle, but this plan totally backfires. Not only does David remain focused in battle to win his bride, but he doubles the number of foreskins. He's now both a soldier and a son-in-law of the king.

2) The Harp and the Spear. (1 Samuel 18)

David keeps his harp, a hobby from his sheep-tending days, and plays for the king's court. King Saul ends up catching an "evil spirit from God" so David plays music to calm him. [22] This works, except for the two times Saul goes psychotic and throws his spear at David.

I have to give David some credit here. I don't think it's an accident that we're told David was almost killed *twice*. It means

---

[22] I've never fully comprehended what this means. Some scholars say that when Saul disobeyed God, that Saul traded the Spirit of God for a spirit of evil (1 Samuel 16:14). Some say that Saul developed a sort of mental illness because of his jealousy and insecurity, perhaps as God's wrath. And some say this was God's last resort so that Saul might turn to God again (1 Corinthians 5:5). However we look at it: King Saul is both struggling and selfish. I feel bad for him, but he also gets what's coming. He is both woefully tragic and tragically wrong.

David went back to Saul after the first time. I doubt I could do the same thing. David remembers the king has accepted him as a son, a soldier, and a bedside musician, even when the king is disturbed enough to kill him. David somehow sees the best in King Saul.

3) They get Saul's goat. (1 Samuel 19)

King Saul hatches a murder plot to take out David, but David's wife Michal gets wind of it and helps him escape. The king's men attempt to kill David in bed, but Michal has this one covered, too. She puts some goat hair on the head of a wooden decoy and leaves it under the sheets. I think I used this trick once in high school to sneak out. I can just imagine the soldiers coming back to King Saul: "My lord, we thrust our swords into the bed of David, but he has turned into a wooden goat."

If Michal was so willing to help David escape the king's wrath, I have to assume their marriage wasn't merely for show. Though there are conflicting interpretations of their marriage, Michal didn't have to help; it would've been to her advantage to let her father win.[23] She warns David first and goes the extra mile on the fake-out. In a time when marriages were arranged for convenience and the annexation of power, here we see a romance that defied both the culture and a murderous king. I

---

[23] Some scholars have said only Michal loved David and it was never reciprocated, or that Michal wanted to save David to become the queen. It's possible. But there's the fact that David took out two-hundred Philistines to win her, double the amount that was requested. There's also that goat-hair statue, which was wholly unnecessary. The one certainty is that their marriage does end badly. Both David and Michal become different people by 2 Samuel 3.

could be over-analyzing, but it seems the heart of David was beyond opportunistic profit.

4) The Arrow and the Moon. (1 Samuel 18, 19, 20)

In the midst of these trials and changes, David becomes best friends with Jonathan, the son of King Saul. We're told they make a *covenant*, an unbreakable bond of loyalty that's the same word used for God's self-initiated love towards us. Jonathan even gives David his sword, bow, belt, and tunic. The tunic is a symbol of the kingdom of Israel, which means Jonathan was giving royal status to David in submission to him. Jonathan firmly wants David to know, "I'm the heir but you should be king. I never want this to get between us."

When Jonathan finds out his father has put a hit on David (the one that ends with the goat-haired trap), Jonathan challenges the order. It's a big deal to oppose the king, even if you're his son. Yet King Saul swears an oath that he won't kill David. Of course, David doesn't believe this, so he and Jonathan conspire to draw out Saul's motives.

There's a New Moon Festival, an important monthly celebration of God's goodness, where David has been invited. David decides to hide out in a field and tells Jonathan, "If your dad gets mad that I'm gone, then he definitely wants me dead." Jonathan says, "If he's fine, I'm going to shoot an arrow close to me. If he's angry, I'll shoot an arrow close to you."

Just as predicted, King Saul explodes at Jonathan and even throws a spear at his own son. David's fears are confirmed. Jonathan returns to the field. An arrow is shot beyond David.

They meet. David bows to the ground three times, and they tearfully embrace. Jonathan tells his friend:

"Go in peace, for we have sworn friendship with each other in the name of the LORD, *saying, 'The* LORD *is witness between you and me, and between your descendants and my descendants forever.'"* (20:42)

They part, uncertain they would ever see each other again.

In this blur of uncontrollable events in David's life, the friendship between David and Jonathan is one of the most powerful stories to come out of the Old Testament. It stands in relief to the typical friendships we hear about in Scripture. Dysfunctional relationships abound: Cain and Abel, Jacob and Esau, Leah and Rachel, Moses and Aaron, Samson and Delilah, Esther and Xerxes. When even an ounce of trial or temptation seeped in, most of these relationships crumbled and collapsed. But David and Jonathan, despite a father who divided them and a kingdom between them, in a time when life was cheap and betrayals were the norm, remained the most intimate of friends to the end. They had every reason to leave: but they stayed.

David's life grew worse and worse, and while most people check out when the going gets tough: Jonathan remains in both the blessing and the mess.

CHAPTER 3
I AM SECOND PLACE:
ABOUT FRIENDSHIP

"You will be king over Israel, and I will be second to you."

1 Samuel 21-23

THE DRAMATIS PERSONAE —

- David, local war hero and prophesied king

- King Saul, the current king, in fear of losing his throne

- Jonathan, the son of King Saul and David's best friend

- Ahimelech, the high priest of the City of Nob

- Doeg, an Edomite mercenary under King Saul

A Race of Thrones:
The Sword of Legend, the Courageous Priest, and the Massacre of the City of Nob

"And even my own son betrays me!" he fumed, throwing the goblet from his veiny fist to the floor. It clattered, splashed, and rolled in circles as the advisors watched. There was a pause, the only sound the cup scratching on its edge in the royal court.

"My lord," an advisor said, jumping at his own voice. "We went after our enemy's mother and father, as you requested. He has hidden them away. The last we heard, he was cowering in the Caves of Adullam, but it is an impossible search."

"Oh, impossible," Saul said, twisting in his throne. "A phantom, you are saying. A ghost-man. Perhaps you, all of you are in this, you scheming, heathen, ungrateful —"

"I have seen David, son of Jesse, my lord," a voice called.

King Saul sat up, adjusting his robes. "Who speaks?"

"It is your servant, Doeg the Edomite." Doeg slid across the cobblestone, armor clinking, to the center of the court square. He was a mercenary who had switched allegiance from Edom to serve under Saul. Half the motive was survival; the other half was wanting to be on the winning side. He had just returned from the high priest's temple, in full battle gear, bronze boots to breastplate, a thin scimitar at his side.

"Leave us," the king said. The advisors rushed off to the chambers on each side. Saul clenched his teeth and drew a breath. "You have my ear, servant."

"He has taken refuge in Nob," Doeg whispered, "with the priest Ahimelech."

"How can I be sure this is true?" Saul said, leaning in. "An accusation against a high priest is of no small consequence."

Doeg licked his lips. "Ahimelech has shared with David the holy bread of the temple, and furthermore ... he has handed him the Sword of Heaven."

"The Sword of Heaven?"

"The sword that beheaded Goliath, my lord. David's first weapon."

Saul turned and closed his eyes. This was ugly. He didn't want to invade the temple. He didn't want to interrogate the priest. But David had gained the confidence of a holy man, enough to surpass the temple rules of consecrated bread, and he had armed himself. With no less than the sword that finished Goliath.

"My lord, there are rumors."

Saul opened his eyes. "Rumors?"

"David is building an army. Only the poor and the discontent have joined, my lord. It is not strong, and they number only in the hundreds."

"You are wrong, Edomite. The discontent are stronger; the smaller are easily impassioned."

"As you say, my lord. It is all the more reason to question Ahimelech."

Saul stared at his fallen cup, the wine in a dash of red across the stones.

"Let it be done. You will travel with me, Doeg. Lead the unit to the City of Nob."

—

Abiathar peered into his father's study.

"Father?"

"Yes, my son," Ahimelech said.

"The king is here to see you."

"So, he is."

Ahimelech the high priest stood to his feet. He fitted the yellow linen ephod across his chest and he glanced to heaven, knowing what was to come.

The soldiers were already inside the temple. A semi-circle of men opened up and King Saul emerged, followed by a man with a scimitar. Ahimelech recognized the man as Doeg, the mercenary who had made a big show of ceremonial cleansing.

King Saul stepped to Ahimelech's nose, close enough for his breath to smother him. "Listen now, son of Ahitub."

"Your servant is listening, my lord."

"Why have you conspired against me, you and the son of Jesse, giving him bread and a sword and inquiring of God for him, so that he has rebelled against me and lies in wait for me?"

Ahimelech pressed both hands to his ephod, touching the sacred garb for strength. He boomed, "Who of all your servants is as loyal as David, the king's son-in-law, captain of your bodyguard and highly respected in your household? Was that day the first time I inquired of God for him? Of course not. Let not the king accuse your servant or any of his father's family, for your servant knows nothing at all about this whole affair."

The king stepped back. "You are as good as dead, priest." Saul motioned to the soldiers. "He has let our enemy go. Kill him as he stands. And the priests, too."

Ahimelech squeezed his garment and nodded at the men. He was ready for death, to go home.

The soldiers gripped the hilts of their swords — but not one of them stepped forward. They looked at one another, at the king, at the priest, and could not move.

"Very well," Saul said. "Doeg, loyal chosen, strike down this priest and his companions."

Doeg unsheathed his scimitar, took one step, and swung across the neck of Ahimelech. Blood fell; the soldiers winced. Before Ahimelech could hit the ground, Doeg wiped his blade on the edge of his tunic and paced to the nearest chamber in the temple. He lifted his blade to strike down the next priest.

There were no screams. Only their prayers, and the mercenary's footsteps between each swing of the scimitar.

—

"My lord David, this man has come from the City of Nob. He says he is the only survivor of a great massacre in his city Perpetrated by the king."

David looked up from the fire, the light dancing with shadows in the woods. The night had been unusually quiet. The reconnaissance had no news of Saul's whereabouts; they had managed to stay a few moves ahead. Until now. David felt the familiar lurch in his stomach, the tightening in his chest, the mix of anger and affection he had for King Saul. This moment was mostly anger. A massacre could only mean that Saul was scorching the earth to find him.

"Let him through," David said.

The guard signaled. Several of David's soldiers marched a young man wearing sacred vestments to the fire. They were stationed in the Forest of Hereth, over four-hundred men and quite a few women, taking refuge in the ancient oaks of Judah.

The embers flickered across the young man's face.

"I know you," David said. "You are the son of Ahimelech. You are called Abiathar."

"Yes, my lord. That is how I found you, through my father. I have come to tell you that ..." Abiathar fell to his knees, weeping. "My father, and the priests. The entire city has been slaughtered."

The surrounding men and women gasped. A few tore their clothes and wept aloud. Abishai, Asahel, and Joab, David's nephews and his best soldiers, screamed and pounded their fists.

Abiathar continued, "The women and children, our cattle and sheep ... even our infants, my lord." There were more cries. "The Edomite under Saul has killed them all."

David fell to his knees, too. He beat his chest and placed both hands on Abiathar. David's hands shook and his voice trembled. "That day, when the Edomite was there ... It is my doing. I alone am responsible for the death of your father. For your whole family. Your city." He began to weep with the priest.

"My lord, it is a burden that you would—"

"No, Abiathar." David held tighter. "Stay with me. With us. Do not be afraid. The man who is seeking your life is seeking mine also. You will be safe with me."

"My lord, I am honored, but I am not a soldier. I have no value here."

David placed a hand on Abiathar's ephod.

"You are a priest," David said. "Even if you were not, you are my family now. Join us. Speak with the Lord on our behalf, for victory. We will fight together."

The campfire pulsed and swirled, as David and his men grieved for the fallen.

If the king wanted war: it was on.

A Loyal Hand: A Love That Never Leaves, Even (and Especially) When It Gets Ugly

This whirlwind of awful events ends with King Saul pursuing David for at least the next four years.[24] I've had to run for my life before, but I can't imagine living with that fear every second, chased by a band of bloodthirsty men that could be just around the corner.

It would be hard to know who to trust. For all David knows, any new person in his army could be a spy or a traitor. They would only need to sneak into David's tent at night and nick his throat with a thumbnail. His soldiers could also leave if things turned bad; King Saul has the superior army and weaponry, and

---

[24] Some scholars say it could be up to fifteen years.

they far outnumber and outclass David's little rogue group of underdogs. David's people had declared their trust, but when the chips were down: who knew?

Our world today is very different, but so much the same.

We live within David's tension. When we're cornered, busted up, and beaten down: who can we really trust? Who will really stay when things get ugly?

Because in the midst of turbulent, unpredictable times, this is what we need —

Someone who will stay.

David's men had every reason to leave him; he played Robin Hood which made them vulnerable. There's a moment after the Massacre of Nob where David saves the City of Keilah from the Philistines, but he ends up exposing his position. Saul bears down and is nearly neck and neck with David in the mountains of the Desert of Ziph. There might have been days when both groups camped on the same hill.

I would understand if David's men left. I might have left, too.

In the middle of this craziness: Jonathan, David's best friend, secretly breaks ranks and goes to David to encourage him.

Now if you were David: Would you still trust Jonathan, the son of the king? The son of the very man who's after your head?

Yet Jonathan has nothing to gain by moving toward David — if anything, it's a death sentence. And David remembers that he and Jonathan had made a covenant. It was a promise of loyalty, *no matter what,* and David trusts that promise.

In 1 Samuel 23, we're told:

And Saul's son Jonathan went to David at Horesh and helped him find strength in God. "Don't be afraid," he said. "My father Saul will not lay a hand on you. You will be king over Israel, and I will be second to you. Even my father Saul knows this." (V.16)

I've always loved these two verses. It's in this friendship that we see the very fabric of our purpose and existence. This might sound like I'm over-stating, but as Timothy Keller says:

"Ultimate reality is a community of persons who know and love one another. That is what the universe, God, history, and life is all about. If you favor money, power, and accomplishment over human relationships, you will dash yourself on the rocks of reality.

"... We believe the world was made by a God who is a community of persons who have loved each other for all eternity. We were made for mutually self-giving, other-directed love. Self-centeredness destroys the fabric of what God has made." [25]

If we're made to love God and love one another, then having and becoming a friend must be one of the highest priorities of our lives. Friendship is different than the general idea of "loving your neighbor." It can't be done with just anyone. It's a unique kind of bond that's both highly selective and widely vulnerable; it has a narrow gate but a broad road. You can open your time and your service to just about anybody, but to open every part of your ugliness, dreams, passions, and insecurities is a colossal risk. It feels like letting someone walk through your ribcage, or giving someone your rib.

---

[25] Timothy Keller, *The Reason for God* (NY: Penguin, 2008) p. 216

You might be surprised there isn't much talk about friendship in the church or in pop culture. The few things we hear are all mixed up with sentimentality or pseudo-masculine language. It's often a concept we take for granted, until we realize how hard it really is and how much it requires wisdom.

And as cheesy as it sounds, *we need friends.* We need partners on this journey. Every other longing in your life is caused by an imperfect world of pain, but the ache of loneliness is the only pain we were made with since the beginning.[26] Life is meant to be lived together, in intense, face-to-face, grace-drenched communion.

This passage in Scripture tells us four things about the friendship between David and Jonathan, but even more importantly, the groundwork of who we want to become and who we want to be around.

Their bond was built on four simple truths.

Love First, Even If, You Too, and *Me Too.*

These are both means and ends. It isn't merely practical or functional, but the bedrock of healthy people who are traveling on the same road together.

---

[26] Genesis 2, when God says, "It is not good for the man to be alone." I first heard the idea of *righteous loneliness* from Timothy Keller in his sermon about spiritual friendship.

- Love First -

Jonathan could've told David, "Let's split up the Kingdom. You take the north and I'll take the south. My dad is king, so I'll take the bigger half. You're good at war so be my general, and I'll do the politics and get the nice chair." It would've been reasonable.

But Jonathan clearly says, *"I will be second to you."*

This is similar to what Apostle Paul writes a thousand years later to the Philippians: *Do nothing out of selfish ambition or vain conceit, but in humility consider others better than yourselves. Each of you should look not only to your own interests, but also to the interests of others.*

It sounds romantic, but putting yourself second goes against our entire nature. None of us have the reflex to "consider others better than ourselves" or to seek someone's interest above our own. The moment we walk into a cafe, we're already evaluating if it's the right temperature and the optimal place to sit and if we'll come back again. No one usually thinks, *How can I help right now? Who can I serve? What can I do to better the place and people around me?* We do the same at work, at home, in the church.

Our default setting is to think, *What's in it for me?*

It's understandable. The human norm is to treat all relationships as **contracts**, which says, "I'll do for you if you do for me." It's a Market of Transaction. There's a kind of safety when you can keep a regulated score, and I think it can be a good thing. We need contracts because there are too many users and abusers who take advantage of the poor sap who wants nothing back.

The problem is that when *every* relationship has an agenda, we dehumanize each other into props and we enslave ourselves to performance. We throw people away or squeeze them dry. We end up too controlling or being controlled. It's the very reason we use and abuse in the first place.

The **covenant** between David and Jonathan is a *just-because love*. It doesn't measure who paid for the last meal. It doesn't grade based on networking or emotional fulfillment. It doesn't count how much can be lost or gained. It exists, *just because*. It chooses to put the other person first. This is the last thing we want to do because it feels so risky: but by choosing to love freely, it's the only thing that will set us free. When we're no longer afraid of outliving our usefulness, we become free to enjoy each other instead of performing to keep each other.

A covenant makes you more human; a contract makes you less. One sees the best in someone; the other draws out the worst.

This isn't just about friendship, but a better world. The only way to build towards harmony is to approach each other without score-cards. It's how we quit chasing after thrones and crowns and names: because when I no longer see people as props for my bidding, I'm no longer imprisoned by my own tyranny. I wouldn't be controlled by my failed attempts at control.

You can actually see Contract and Covenant everywhere in these verses. David's wife Michal helped David escape Saul's men. Ahimelech kept David in his temple, feeding him consecrated bread, and stayed true to David at the threat of his own life. David built an army of people who were societal outcasts, not evaluating their skills or wealth. In contrast, Doeg the Edomite sold out the priest to get on the king's good side. And of course, King Saul was so insecure over his throne that he pursued David with the full force of the military.

I don't mean to pit one against the other. Most earthly relationships won't be just-because covenants; a contract is inevitable and necessary. But we do need at least the one friend who we can laugh with like an idiot or weep with like a baby. I need the friend around who I'm free to just *be,* without trying to impress or measure up. That's one of the unique parts about friendship: we sing and dance for the world to get something, but a friend means you just *get them.* It's a trust that you can fail and they'll still be around in the morning, and it creates a strength and security like nothing else can.

Jonathan is in line to be the king, but he's not bound to the crown. He cared first about David's life and future. I've met people with this kind of devoted transparency, a person who wasn't always working an angle. It's rare. But their presence is so incredibly warm and appealing that it makes me stronger when I'm around them. I feel safe enough to drop my guard and put away the merchandise. With most people, I'm tense because they pull and demand and expect — but there's that one person who only wants to know if I'm okay, and those are the people I draw near. They love first, without small print, and that's who I want to be, too.

I want to make sure that I don't mislead you with the word "love." A covenant kind of love isn't just about being "nice." The first thing Jonathan says to David is, *"Don't be afraid."* This was an emphatic command. It was counter to David's reality, because he was on the run and afraid all the time. But David needed that other voice, the one who wasn't going to pamper or coddle. David needed encouragement as well as a stronger spine.

To be loving means both restoration and rebuke. It embraces and empowers. It melts our fears and galvanizes us into action.

As harsh as this sounds: If you haven't been told you're wrong in a long time, you probably have no real friends and you might not be a great friend, either, because everyone's too scared to tell you what's real. Even the most mature of us have a hard time with rebuke; I've never met a single person who handled it very well, including me. Yet true friends are willing to put the friendship on the line out of love for each other. Putting your friend first will often mean putting your comfort second. Good friends are willing to push past the initial emotional reaction and the defensiveness and all the scratching and hissing of self-preservation. They'll also shut the door on self-pity so you can't escape. It'll hurt, a lot. This is the other unique part about friendship: you can't have accountability with just anyone. It's a big deal when we lend each other the power to call us out on our selfish tendencies.

It doesn't mean we call out everything that bothers us. There's plenty to just let go. I don't mean we're behavior-police or try to catch a slip-up all the time. Being accountable is nothing without grace and vision, and if you have a self-satisfying relish when you rebuke, you're not in it for your friend, but yourself. None of this is about ultimatums or "getting things off my chest." It's because I love you too much to stay silent.

This is a heartbreaking process, because for every uncomfortable truth-session I've had with a friend, I've lost about half that many. When I look back, there were plenty of friends who tried to be truthful with me when it didn't benefit them, but I refused to listen. I'm starting to understand that being a friend is not a fun-filled fantasy that fits my every whim. It's not for my entertainment. We cannot grow by surrounding ourselves with yes-men and people-pleasers. Friends sharpen one another, to be our truest, best selves, that we might move forward to greater joy.

We need a voice that both relieves and rebukes.

Love means I have to tell you everything, even if my voice trembles and my hands shake and my eyes burn with weeping.

Love means I will throw my body in front of you when you're heading towards the cliff.

It will cost my comfort with you.

It's a cost I'm willing to pay.

Proverbs 17:17 – A friend loves at all times,
and a brother is born for adversity.
27:17 – As iron sharpens iron,
so one man sharpens another.

27:6 – Wounds from a friend can be trusted,
but an enemy multiplies kisses.
15:31 – He who listens to a life-giving rebuke
will be at home among the wise.

"The Christian needs another Christian who speaks God's Word to him. He needs him again and again when he becomes uncertain and discouraged, for by himself he cannot help himself without belying the truth." [27]
— Dietrich Bonhoeffer

- <u>Even If</u> -

Even though David had just outed his location, Jonathan came to see him anyway.

I hope we see how huge this really is. David is considered social poison. Jonathan had most likely heard about the Massacre of Nob, and if the king could slay an entire temple of priests and a city full of children, he might not hesitate at his own son.

But Jonathan went to the Untouchable.

I've been the Untouchable before. What I mean is, a rumor would fly around and people that I called friends suddenly called me a liability. I've suffered from clinical depression for as long as I can remember, and for some, this is too much to endure. I've had a past and I've been in the same town for a long time, so quite a few people are allergic to my sin. It's a horrible thing to

[27] Dietrich Bonhoeffer, *Life Together* (NY: HarperCollins, 1954) p. 7

believe that you'll never get past what you've done or what you've gone through.

The rare few said, *Even if you've messed up and you're a mess and you've done messy things — I'll stay. I'll get in your mess.*

Jonathan became an accomplice. If he was caught with David, they would've been executed together. Essentially, Jonathan became poison, too. In order to strengthen David, Jonathan had to become weak by association.

This sort of love is a *substitution,* and that's what love is. *Real love is a self-sacrificial effort of pouring out your life for another.* It's to become the other person and walk in their shoes. It's to switch places.

You've seen this before. A popular kid in high school befriends the outcast, and the outcast gets a little more cred while the popular kid loses his. When you counsel an unstable person, you pour out some of your stability which strengthens them but weakens you. A mother and father make enormous sacrifices for their child to see them prosper. When meerkats graze in the field, there's always a sentry that will warn the others when a hawk or a wolf draws near, and the sentry usually gets eaten so the family can survive. All love is substitution.[28] All friendship is substitution on a two-way street.

Most people won't go for *Even-If* love because it's so draining. I get it; there should definitely be a pacing and wisdom and

---

[28] The first three examples were borrowed from Timothy Keller.

proper navigation about it. But the end result is always two stronger people, because one of the inverse truths about pouring out is that you get filled up. The friends who check out early get stagnant later in life because it became a habit to run. There's no chance for depth. Two friends who persevere always solidify a bond from all that came before. It drills deep. By staying, it makes us better than we had any right to be.

This isn't just about difficult times. Friends also stay when the difficult thing is each other. *Even if you mess it up with me, I'll forgive you.* On a long enough timeline, two imperfect people are going to hurt each other, but an *Even-If* kind of love also loves through pain. As a pastor once said, "There can be no enduring relationships without forgiveness."[29]

There are friendships I've mourned over where too much history got in the way. There were too many harsh words and broken promises and silent disagreements, and it rotted to an impatient grave. But there are others where we traveled the jagged road of reconciliation, mending wounds and untying knots and covering with grace, and on the other end of this is an ocean-deep intimacy of perseverance that couldn't be reached any other way. We had to wrestle with the ugly parts of our nature. Demons were exposed. Secrets were spilled.

Yet there is a joy in this sort of enduring friendship that goes the long distance. There's a crazy sort of laughter with a lifelong friend that is colored by the weight of heels digging into the

---

[29] The first time I heard this was from James MacDonald MacDonald in his sermon series, "Always Resolve Everything Now," preached at Harvest Bible Chapel in Chicago, IL.

ground, a love that says, "I'm staying." We see it in the cross, and we can have it now, even in a world such as this.

- You Too / Me Too -

Jonathan, by going to David, was essentially saying: "In trouble? Then me, too."

It was C.S. Lewis who put it so wonderfully:

"Friendship is born at that moment when one person says to another: 'What! You too? I thought I was the only one.'" [30]

From this, a definition of friendship could be: *A mutual bond of trust with common interests going in the same direction, to bring out the very best.*

When my friend is hurt, I can say, "You, too? Me, too."

When my friend is offensive or immature, I can say, "You, too? Me, too."

When I have to be truthful with my friend about their issues, I have to examine myself first. Because maybe it's me, too.

When my friend is in the valley and the desert, then it's me, too.

If my friend is passionate about something, then it's important to me, too, because it's important to my friend. I don't have to get it, but I don't have to bash it.

---

[30] C.S. Lewis, *The Four Loves* (FL: Harcourt, 1960, 1988) p. 78. This is a redaction of the quote which has been posted by C.S. Lewis' official social media accounts. The original quote says, "Friendship, I have said, is born at that moment when one man says to another 'What! You too? I thought that no one but myself ...'"

I can rejoice with those who rejoice, and mourn with those who mourn.[31]

I will either be the voice that helps someone overcome, or the voice they must overcome.

Whether my friend is struggling or selfish, pretentious or passionate, or hurting or harmful, I can always say, "You, too? Me, too."

It isn't easy, but this kind of approach can solve about a million problems. When my wife and I get in an argument, I tend to trump up what *she* did wrong while I play up what *I* did right. It's a horrible, insulating process that only reinforces my pride and dissolves my humanity. I tend to say that the things I did wrong were "out of my control" while the things she did wrong were flaws in her character.

I forget that both of us do wrong because of the deeper fractures inside us that manifest as friction, and often it's not about "me against her," but a fundamental wound that's threaded in our nature. The second I can say *You-Too/Me-Too*, then I quit my superiority and we stand as equals and I can bring my own wrong to the surface, no matter how small it might be. I can approach the actual problem instead of attacking the person. It immediately makes me human again, and I can see my wife as a friend on a journey instead of an enemy that I have to conquer.

This is how we stay when we most want to leave: by celebrating the best in each other and owning up to the ugly parts of

---

[31] Romans 12:15

ourselves, so that we can share these joys and burdens for the very long road ahead. It's also how we become the best people we can be.

One of my favorite quotes about this sort of approach is from Stephen Colbert, in a commencement speech he did for Northwestern University.

"After I graduated from here, I moved down to Chicago and did improv. Now there are very few rules to improvisation, but one of the things I was taught early on is that you are not the most important person in the scene. Everybody else is. And if they are the most important people in the scene, you will naturally pay attention to them and serve them. But the good news is you're in the scene too. So hopefully to them you're the most important person, and they will serve you. No one is leading, you're all following the follower, serving the servant. You cannot win improv.

"... So no more winning. Instead, try to love others and serve others, and hopefully find those who love and serve you in return." [32]

---

[32] Colbert's Commencement Address 2011,
http://www.northwestern.edu/newscenter/stories/2011/06/colbert-speech-text.html

Our True Friend:
The Infinite Wellspring

The hard part about loving people is the whole thing. It sounds fun until you actually try it. You know the roommate story: two best friends decide to room together and then they find out what they're *really* like, and they leave as bitter enemies. Lifelong friendship is a cute idea until you're pulling your hair out over dirty dishes, towels on the floor, late rent payments, and grudges that poison the well. High school can seem like forever until you open your yearbook to the empty, forgotten signatures. Old married couples seem sweet until you get on the inside and hear about the lonely nights in the same bed, the temptations, the arguments that nearly ended it all. And no one wants to deal with the friend who's emotionally unstable, overly needy, and a downright drag.

Maybe that person is you. It's certainly been me.

Sometimes I see a friendship like David's and Jonathan's, or a fifty-year marriage, or the Bible's commands on how to be a good friend, and I get discouraged that *I can't do this. It's not in me. I'm too weird and messed up and ugly in here.*

It takes a miracle to be a friend and stay a friend. Relational intimacy requires a supernatural muscle that's far beyond us. In order to be an anchor, we need an anchor first.

When Jonathan goes to David, he doesn't say, "Trust me, I got you." First Samuel 23:16 says Jonathan *"helped [David] find strength in God."*

The Hebrew words there are, *Jonathan strengthened his hand in God.*

As David and Jonathan gripped hands, they were first gripped by the very hands of God. Yet as David and Jonathan had to part, God never did.

It was in such security that they could strengthen one another. They started with a vertical love before it was horizontal. They didn't squeeze from each other what only God could give. Their love was the surplus of abundance that they had in God Himself.

Maybe this sounds a bit trite to you, but we need this so much more than you think. There's no human friend who can possibly bear the entire brunt of our burdens and expectations. No one can be everything we need them to be all the time. We often wring others dry of their encouragement, affirmation, and investment, but they're just people, too, and they need the same wellspring as you do. Even more: You cannot possibly fulfill your friend at every turn. You cannot play savior for long, and there's no end to pleasing people. Everyone will demand a piece of your soul that will fall short anyway.

When I believe God will never leave, then I'm already complete. I can love someone without really *needing* them. I'm not squeezing affirmation or salvation from others. They're not merely supporting roles for the movie of my life, but gifts to be honored and cherished. I can also meet my friend's demands without bowing down to them, because I'm no longer afraid of their disapproval. It would be nice to cater to the majority or my parents or my roommate, but I cannot abide in their opinions of me. *"With you, I am well pleased,"* the Father said of Jesus, and says of us, too.[33]

In the end, *God is the only please-able one*, because He has preemptively accepted us in the full grace of His Son, and His opinion is the first and last one we need. This is the wellspring that not only fills us, but allows our overflow to fill others. Nothing less than the love of God could get us to love like He does.

Those who are loved much will love much.[34]

We also find that not only does God empower us to be a friend, but that God *is* a friend.[35] Jonathan came to David in the middle of the mess and literally said, "Death will not find you." This is a lightning-bolt of the Gospel in the darkness of the Old Testament. David could not have known that Jonathan was a picture of such future grace.

We have that picture now fully realized. We believe Jesus came to us in the middle of our mess — and didn't just strengthen our hand in God, but *was* the strength of God. He also said, "Death will not find you," and though he had the right to be the King, he instead gave us the right to his crown and his inheritance. Jesus gave us his royalty, but even more, stood in the way of death by taking it on. While Jonathan was risking his life, Jesus gave his life. Jonathan was an accomplice, but Jesus was a

---

[33] Matthew 3:17, Mark 1:11, Luke 3:22, 2 Peter 1:17
[34] Luke 7:47
[35] John 15:14, James 2:23

scapegoat. In a sense, Jesus switched places with us. He was the ultimate substitution, once and for all, and it was he who knew no sin who became sin for us.[36]

We have the perfect friend, Jesus Christ, who *can* bear the brunt of our entire soul, and did. He wholly loved first, even if, and as God wrapped in flesh, said, *You, too? Me, too.* He saw the ugliness of our hearts and stayed.

God is absolutely vast and holy, but He's also as close as your spouse and your roommate and your best friend. Both realities are true. Jesus can lead us, but he is with us. He is bigger than our comprehension, yet closer than our hearts. He stayed above temptation but suffered through our trials. He is the Most High King, yet he relates to where we are.

God stepped into the dirt and was tempted, tired, betrayed, beaten, and killed. Jesus wasn't merely crucified, which would've been enough, but shared his entire life with us. No one can say that God doesn't know what we're going through. He does, intimately, with profound depth, even more than we dare to fathom. He *knows.*

No human being on earth can meet such criteria. We have a God who is so glorious that His very sight would ruin us, but by His grace, we have Him face-to-face, in the peaks and valleys, through success and failure, in loneliness and wandering — with kindness instead of judgment, as every friend does.

---

[36] 2 Corinthians 5:21

He is like no other friend, yet the friend we've always wanted.
He will walk with you when no one else will.

"I no longer call you servants,
because a servant does not know his master's business.
Instead, I have called you friends,
for everything that I learned from my Father
I have made known to you."
— Jesus, John 15:15

A Word For You:
Be the Cheerleader

I've learned that the quickest thing that kills friendships is
jealousy. Sometimes it's a slow death; jealous people can act
loving for a lifetime, but they waste their lives comparing to each
other instead of helping each other out.

We have one man, King Saul, who is insecure over his name,
and he wants to kill David. We have another man, Jonathan, son
of the king in line for the throne, yet he wants to crown David.

I think Saul could've easily befriended David and nurtured his
gifts. He could've taught David and poured into him and
discipled him to be a future leader. Of course, Saul was older and
would've had a slightly different role than a friend, but the truth
remains: *Jealousy can cut short the empowering work of friendship and all*
the joy and vision it brings forth.

I'm either your cheerleader or the loop of condemnation in your head. And I know which one I prefer to be around.

I hate what jealousy does to people. The worst, most cutting words come from envy. Families, churches, and businesses rot from the inside. It causes even the nicest people to horde their own talents and hold others back, and they'd rather snuff out the torch then pass it on to a new generation. It turns us into small, shrewish versions of ourselves.

I've lost friends this way, and you can't really call someone out on jealousy. It feels arrogant. No one confesses it, either. In my years of ministry, I've never heard someone tell me, "I'm just a jealous, insecure hater." Have you ever said that in the mirror? Me, neither. You'll hear about murder and drugs in the confession booth before envy. It blinds us into denial.

Jonathan promoted his friend's potential to see his very best. This makes Jonathan sound like some kind of sugary pushover, but I'm sure it wasn't so easy for Jonathan. Some of his dad's envy could've caught him in sleepless nights. Maybe Jonathan flinched a little when the townspeople sang about David in the streets. And I think that's okay. Jealousy is going to happen because it's part of being in a fallen world: so what will we do when it comes?

Preparation is half the battle. If you name the demon, you have a better chance of beating it. Fighting sin means expecting the monster, and then tackling it in the doorway. It means laying down the worldly weapon to pick up a weapon of grace.

Jonathan went against the reflex of his flesh to say, *I will be second to you.*

Jonathan decided not to be jealous *of* David, but *for.*

It really does warm my heart to see this. I've seen a lot of good friends get blown up when envy got a foothold. One friend would get successful in their field while the other stayed unseen, and the unseen friend starts to feel like their famous friend owes them. There's a lot of fist-shaking at God and self-directed anger. It's nasty stuff.

When you're good at something, be ready. You'll fast become a threat to others. It won't be just "haters" or "trolls." You'll get shot down from your closest loved ones when you get slightly better. But even then, we can receive the criticism and dismiss the parts that are petty. We can keep using our talents to serve those who are mad. Like David, we play the harp for the guy who hates us. After all, the best way to beat jealousy is to hold your gifts with a loose hand, because you're showing that your ability isn't something to horde, but to give. All of it was given to you anyway.

And if you're a bit like me, who sort of feels behind everyone and is a very late bloomer, I hope we're self-aware enough to celebrate our friends who are more successful and talented. Many of them worked hard to get there and there's a lot to learn from them. It's okay if you and I are not as "good" as someone else or have "less" ability. We can still promote the less skilled and the newly started, since we have much to offer to them, too.

Imagine if every time you felt jealousy or took it hard on yourself: you instead took joy in someone's gifting and you were able to enjoy it for what it is.

Imagine if every time a friend did something amazing in the world, you were to ask them, "How did you do it? What did it take you to get there? How did God help you in this? How can I keep praying for you?"

Imagine if you were to find out your friend was really wrestling with their sudden success, and you could be their counsel.

Maybe you and I would find, *It's not about me all the time.*

And we could love first, even if.

You, too? Me, too.

CHAPTER 4
YOUR LIFE IS
PREACHING A MESSAGE

"The LORD delivered you into my hands today, but I would not lay a hand on the LORD's anointed."

1 Samuel 24 and 26

Getting Even Against All Odds

David gets the perfect opportunity to kill King Saul. Twice. They've been locked in a chase for years now, and Saul happens to stop by a cave where David and his men are hiding.

Saul starts peeing. David and his men can't believe what they're seeing.

It seems that fate and the stars and planets have aligned, as if God is giving Saul over to David. David's men prod him. He's probably prodding himself.

Imagine: Saul walks into a cave, and David walks back out with Saul's head.[37] "Is this your king?" Saul's men fall over in allegiance. They want a king with his head still attached.

---

[37] I borrowed this imagery from Andy Stanley's sermon, "Pay Attention to the Tension."

But David doesn't do this. He instead cuts off a strip of Saul's robe and orders his men to back off. He follows King Saul out of the cave with the strip of cloth and says, *"This day you have seen with your own eyes how the* LORD *delivered you into my hands in the cave. Some urged me to kill you, but I spared you; I said, 'I will not lift my hand against my master, because he is the* LORD*'S anointed.'"*

Saul is stunned. "You are more righteous than I," he says. Saul is so embarrassed that he swears an oath to spare David.

The oath lasts a couple days.

Only a short while later, Saul is at it again. David is camping at the Desert of Ziph and sees Saul and his three-thousand men. At night, David and Abishai sneak over to Saul's sleeping body. Abishai wants to put a spear through him. "I won't strike him twice," he says. But David stops him. *"The* LORD *forbid that I should lay a hand on the* LORD*'S anointed."* David grabs Saul's water jug and spear and runs back.

From a hill, David calls out to Saul's right-hand man Abner. David yells, *"You're a man, aren't you?"* I've always wanted this verse on my wall.

Then David delivers the clincher. *"What you have done is not good. As surely as the* LORD *lives, you and your men deserve to die, because you did not guard your master, the* LORD*'S anointed. Look around you. Where are the king's spear and water jug that were near his head?"*

I'm sure Abner said, "Oh, crap."

Saul wakes up. He's stunned again. He apologizes again. "I have sinned," he says. "I'm sorry about the whole trying-to-kill-you thing." He makes another big show of flattery and leaves with his men.

And Saul means it this time. The chase is over. Saul is apparently a changed man and he quits running after David.

This sounds like a cute story of integrity, but let's consider David's dilemma.

He's been on the run for at least four years. He has a family. His men are tired. They're homeless. One kill and the chase would've been over. Life was cheap back then; this was an ancient barbaric culture where people died in battle all the time. Maybe this sounds awful to you, but if we're to displace ourselves from modern Western sensibilities, it was kill-or-be-killed. In fact, it might have even been right to kill Saul. He had massacred an entire city and he was mentally unfit to be a king. It was to David's every advantage to take him out. It would've been easier to shank Saul in the back and let him bleed out in the cave. Or to punch Saul to death in his sleep.

At a glance, David's actions look merciful and pure. But in the moment, David would've been called stupid. His men could have mutinied or Saul could have eventually killed them all. No one was thinking of "the moral of the story" or "preserving honor."

If I were David — I probably would've turned that cave into Saul's grave.

Everywhere else in the Bible, bad men meet a bad end. We want the same thing in our history books and blockbusters. If I were one of David's men, I would've bothered David all night until he gave in. "You basically shot Goliath, remember? Just one more guy and we'll finally have world peace."

Why spare Saul?

You Have a World Inside You

The thing I admire most about David here is that he had such a huge vision. He wasn't thinking from a trigger-finger. He saw as wide as possible, with every implication and every angle of his decision, stretching out beyond himself.

The murder of Saul would've sent a very specific message to the people of Israel: that it was open season to move up the ladder by blood.

David didn't want the kingdom by force, and a take-over would only promote unrest and instability in Israel. It was no good to win people by killing their king. There was also no guarantee that if David killed Saul, he would automatically get the throne. If he did, he would open himself to someone else doing the same to him. David would go from outrunning Saul to running from his own men, stuck in a kill-or-be-killed cycle for the rest of his life.

It probably sounds like David is a shrewd politician and made a strategic choice, but there's a deeper truth to his actions. *David seized an opportunity to set off a chain reaction of events that could end in reconciliation and righteousness.* It was a long shot, but he took it. He didn't do it for himself. He leveraged any kind of influence he had for the king and for his men, and trusted God to do the part that he couldn't do: to change the hearts there.

David trusted God for the better story.

If it was even slightly possible for Saul to change, David was going to risk it. He was hoping that Saul would be struck by such kindness that he would not only quit hunting David, but become a better man. After all, David had a piece of Saul's robe and his spear and water jug, all exclamation points for Saul's spared life. David was trying to reach any humanity that was still left in the king.

Of course, there was no guarantee that Saul would change.

But killing Saul would guarantee a runaway train of death.

In the end, mercy melts Saul. In Robert Alter's commentary on this passage, he says:

"This is one of those extraordinary reversals that make biblical narrative such a probing representation of the oscillations and the unpredictabilities of human nature: David's words have cut to the quick of the king's conscience, and suddenly the obsessive pursuer feels an access of paternal affection, intertwined with remorse, for his imagined enemy. Saul ... has to shake himself to believe his enemy is his friend, because he stands at a certain distance from David ... and also because his eyes are blinded with tears." [38]

Essentially, David's life had become a sermon. His life was preaching a message that would reverberate upon the contours

---

[38] Robert Alter, *The David Story* (NY: W.W. Norton & Company, 1999) p. 151

of the people and the world around him. It was contrary to everything they did and believed: but by threading such mercy into the tapestry of hardened people, David was inaugurating a different kind of kingdom in the darkness. He was ushering in the first strands of light.

Your life is preaching a message, too.

Your life and my life are leaving footprints for the people behind us and our children ahead of us. There's no doubt that you have imprints left by someone else.

A few years ago, a father named Garth Callaghan began writing inspirational notes on napkins for his fourteen year old daughter to put in her lunchbox. Garth had three separate diagnoses of cancer. He wrote 826 notes for each day that his daughter had left in school. "At the end of the day," he said, "these notes might be the only thing my daughter has left of me."[39]

We're doing the same thing. We're leaving notes everywhere we go. That might sound trite and overly earnest, but the notes you leave really matter.

We're creating a story of the world for ourselves and someone else. It's all a matter of the story you're telling.

---

[39]   http://newsfeed.time.com/2014/01/27/dad-is-prepping-over-800-napkin-notes-for-daughters-lunchbox-before-he-dies/

The Story You Tell Is the Story You Know

Why is this important?

I can tell you why it was important for me. I had spent years living without intentionality and completely disengaged, so most of my choices were spurts of the latest, loudest emotion, and I bought into all kinds of lies that I never investigated down to the bottom. I was pushed around by neon signs and gut instinct and crawling on autopilot. I drank a lot. There are some weeks that are just stains in memory, stretches of my ghost nodding along with the next face I couldn't remember. I was barely living inside my own head. Half the time when I knew *why* I was doing something, it was never for a good reason, and half the time when I knew *what* I was doing, it was never really good. It was all a quiet blur of nothing, and I dragged others with me.

I never dug deep into *Who-I-Am*. I was content to bump around in a hazy, haphazard life. At best, I was unreliable, and at worst, destructive.

But occasionally I met someone like David, like Esther, like Paul, who was so emblazoned with boldness and certainty that it woke me up to bigger possibilities. It wasn't about comparison or insecurity, but admiration for a life well lived: not perfectly, but with passion, for a reason bigger than themselves.

I saw amazing stories, and I knew a secret regret had been growing inside. It's the same regret they tell you about when a person is at the end, on a bed, telling you what they wish they could've done. It's the same regret I had when I survived suicide, waking up to sobriety and no way to escape myself. I was looking for form, for a story to tell, for a coherent purpose so meaningful that I would quit chasing a version of myself and finally feel alive.

I don't say this as a cautionary tale or a guilt trip. Your situation might not be as dreary and dramatic as mine was. But I've met so many of the same kinds of people, who stab at random things and don't know why and are never really depressed, but they don't have much joy or depth, either. Every choice is isolated inside a vacuum of discontinuity with no relation to any previous choice, and there's no sense that this is going anywhere, since it's controlled by the heat of the moment. Even the most successful of us wonder what it's going to mean in the end.

Without a story to tell, we never quite finish well. We never quite finish at all. It is a life of half-finished bridges, and I wanted to cross.

I know that no one wants to tell a bad story with their life, but many of us are not sure how to tell a good one.

Eventually I began to ask:

What's this all for?

Where did I hear that from?

And why do I believe it to be true?

I found that these were terrifying questions, because it meant I couldn't coast anymore and I had to consider the possibility that life was meaningful and I had to find something to live for. It's scary to consider that we're each infused with a unique purpose and a power. *"Our deepest fear is not that we are inadequate. Our deepest fear is that we are powerful beyond measure. It is our light, not our darkness that most frightens us."* [40]

I'm not saying anything new. We all need "something to live for." It's a well-worn cliché by now. But the hard part is actually living for it, without compromise, even when every other voice is screaming at you to do what's easy.

When I see David on the run, he could've easily followed what he felt. His men were practically demanding him to take the easy way out. But David could see wide because he had dug so deep. He knew exactly what he was living for. He stuck to his word. He considered others, but bent to no one. He stayed true.

I find David's reliability so appealing that it hurts. His consistency is almost intimidating.

How did he do it?

I don't think this passage has a simple formula for a consistent life, but there are at least two things we learn from David about how he got there.

The first truth is: **Who-I-am pours out what-I-do.**

It's actually quite a hard thing to say, "I know who I am," especially with a confidence that remains unwavering in the back-and-forth tug of everyone else's opinion. Even if you try to say it

[40] Marianne Williamson, *A Return To Love* (NY: HarperCollins, 1992) p. 190

in the mirror, it's a little more embarrassing than you might think.

Some of us cling to a tenuous cord of who we want to be and there's little continuity about ourselves from day-to-day. That's not a condemnation at you. I know it's really hard to think about these things because we're busy and distracted and pulled in a million directions. At times it feels easier to camouflage our way in to every situation and be a happy little chameleon. I love it when people like me, so I tend to be what people want from me.

But for moments at a time: Who-you-are and the person you *want-to-be* has slammed into you with the force of a freight train, and you stood tall in the wind. You stood resolute with conviction. There are times of razor-sharp focus when everything else whittled away, and you knew exactly what you were about, and you had both a rest and resolve to handle the things in front of you with statuesque fortitude.

It's the same moment that the prodigal son had in Luke 15, when *he came to himself.*

This isn't trick psychology. These are memories of the person who God made you to be, breaking in to your slumber with the aim of a laser-sight, harkening you back to His glory.

Sometimes you remembered yourself. And it was glorious.

David's advantage, as morbid as it sounds, was that he was running for his life. Every moment, he knew *this could be it,* and mortality has a way of crystallizing what's most important. He had to dig deep. He had to ask those questions: *What's this all for? Where did I hear that from? And why do I believe it to be true?* David grew absolutely clear about himself because his constant brush with death forged a meditative intensity that he couldn't avoid. As David hid in deserts and forests and caves, writing psalm after psalm, praying to God in helpless vulnerability, he gained an intimate understanding about who God is and what He is all about.

Even more than that, God had pursued David and found *him*. God had continually revealed Himself by reversing the human ideals of strength and doing the unexpected: He picked a shepherd to be the future king; He worked through a boy to take down a giant; He subverted the jealousy of two friends in line for the same throne. This is the same God who split a sea and saved a nation of nobodies. David continually remembered himself by remembering who God was and what He had done.

This is faith. It's awakening to the reality that our glorious, gracious God has been pursuing you all along, that you'd be intimately one with Him again.

If I were to ask David, "Do you know who you are?" — I imagine that for all his trials and trouble, this is the one thing he would know with assurance.

"I am made for, saved for, and shaped for Him. I know who I am because I know who He is."

David's utmost identity was shaped on the very story of God's upside-down goodness enduring in a hostile world. David believed in a God who could uppercut the worst in people and bring out their best. And this is the same story that David preached with his life.

God is pursuing you too, that you might become in tune with the heart of divinity, to tell His story. It's a hard one to tell, but it's the best one there is.

If you believe your worth comes from God apart from what everyone else says — you'll confer the same worth to others, regardless of what others say.

If you believe true strength comes from the humility and patience of God — you'll be just as humble and patient with others as God was with you.

If you believe real love is found in the substitutionary covenant of Christ — you'll love others for who they are instead of what they can do for you.

The more we can have clarity about God's activity, the more it makes us into who we're meant to be. The more we're saturated in His story, the more we will be as He is.

Remember Him, and you'll remember yourself.

The second truth is: **What-we-do reinforces who-we-are.** This is the harder one because it'll sound like legalism and mechanical faith — but this part is the key to consistency that unlocks a better story.

If you want to be a certain kind of person, you need to do what that kind of person does.

Your nature dictates your behavior, but your behavior promotes your nature.

When David saw Saul in the cave, there was no question in his mind about what to do. David had already made the same kind of decisions hundreds of times. This was one more act of mercy in a long string of mercy.

The entirety of David's choices over his whole life led up to the moment where he showed grace. David had a momentum from every decision he made before; he had been in a continuous stream of wise, right choices from day one. He was taking in the poor and unwanted from every town; he had saved the City of Keilah from the Philistines even when it exposed his position; he had hidden his parents in a refuge so that Saul couldn't reach them. His actions had fortified his heart, so that even when he came across a difficult decision, David had already chosen who he was. He knew the kind of person he wanted to be by the time he got to the scene.

This isn't something you can sculpt in a day. It's not like cramming for an exam or paper. As a pastor once said, "Who you are today is not from what you've done today, but from all you've done before. And who you are tomorrow will come from everything you do today."[41]

The same is true in every commitment you ever make. Marriage requires choosing love even when you don't feel loving. Work requires work even at our worst. Faith is less about feeling God and more about resting in His faithfulness. And as we

[41] I first heard this from Matt Chandler of The Village Church in Flower Mound, TX. I've paraphrased it.

choose each commitment despite ourselves, it creates the necessary motivations and feelings and inspired surges of focus to keep going.

Every subsequent choice fuels another choice, and those choices form a groove in how you choose. As our brother Lewis says, *"Do not waste time bothering whether you 'love' your neighbor; act as if you did. As soon as we do this we find one of the great secrets. When you are behaving as if you loved someone, you will presently come to love him."*

David loved Saul so he let him go, but by letting him go, David loved Saul all the more.

Our identity informs our choices, and our choices circle back on our identity. Faith is the engine and works are the shuttle.

We're both saved from and made for something.

We believe and then we proceed.

The Christian faith is about life being made alive.

"[Every] time you make a choice, you are turning the central part of you, the part of you that chooses, into something a little different from what is was before. And taking your life as a whole, with all your innumerable choices, all your life long you are slowly turning this central thing either into a heavenly creature or a hellish creature: either into a creature that is at harmony with God, and with other creatures, and with itself, or else into one that is in a state of war and hatred with God, and with its fellow creatures, and with itself. To be the one kind of creature is heaven: that is, it is joy and peace and knowledge and power. To be the other means madness, horror, idiocy, rage, impotence, and eternal loneliness. Each of us at each moment is progressing to the one state of the other.

"... Good and evil both increase at compound interest. That is why the little decisions you and I make every day are of such infinite importance. The smallest good act today is the capture of a strategic point from which, a few months later, you may be able to go on to victories you never dreamed of." [42]

— C.S. Lewis

Our True Message:
A Mission Bigger Than the Moment

I am like Saul, chasing down the true king to kill him in a cave, to spear him in his side, so that I can live in my own freedom: when such freedom is aimlessness and my own story isn't big enough to live for.

We need a message and a mission and a story so powerful that it disrupts the grain of our apathy and selfishness. We need a narrative so grand and sweeping that it expels every lesser idol that has taken us hostage. We need a voice bigger than the pampering choir of pointless, prodigal, halfway thrills.

We're creatures of story. We not only need a narrative, but we bleed one, too, and the world you build comes out of the story you believe.

But I believe we have more than a message, a diagram, a flowchart, or even a story.

---

[42] C.S. Lewis, *Mere Christianity* (NY: HarperCollins, 1952, 1980) p. 92, 132

We have a person. We have the perfect author.

He was not spared in a cave, but he emerged as grace.

He was not spared the spear, but he took on such pain.

He reversed death and our sin in a grave.

And such love melted me, that I would not only be forgiven:

But set free for a fruitful, passionate, mission-driven life.

My motive is no longer to preach a better message, but it's that I already have one.

I have Him. More importantly, He has me.

A Word For You:
The Blank Page of a New Door

Right now, you might be ready to turn it all around.

You know exactly who you want to be and what you need to do.

It's going to be tough.

Sometimes you think you know who-you-are, and those trials and temptations rip you apart at the seams. Sometimes we're barely escaping our past and the consequences we've wrought, like pulling our boots from the swamp. Sometimes we're making good progress and our faith is growing and we're doing all the right things, but we relapse and regress and totally fall off a cliff.

We've been more like Saul, having been given a chance — and we squandered it.

The bad news is that none of us are like David.

The good news is that all of us are like Saul.

He got a second chance. I've gotten many. And you will, too. Maybe the door will close on that relationship or city or job: but God doesn't close His door. You can still remember who you are and who you're not.

At that juncture, it's never too late to start again.

I hope you won't inject a false narrative over your life that condemns you to a time-stamp. I hope you won't believe the lie that "I am what I've done" or "I am what's been done to me." You're not doomed to the memory-loop of what happened before. Of course, we must take responsibility for our poor choices, and we can't deny where we're guilty — but it's no good living in a constant apology, trying to pay off the guilt with pious self-punishment. The consequences are your *Time Served.* You don't have to keep hanging your head in shame to display how bad you feel.

You can get off the devil's script and reboot your story again. As much as you've heard it before: you really can own your part and get on a new chapter.

It might mean that you go back to apologize. To make it right and reconcile. To cut off the comfortable. To confess your crimes, even at the cost of your name. To finally let go of the things that hold you back and grab the grace-driven discipline to begin again. To finally ask the hard questions about who you really are and where you're really going, and to get back on the axis of divinity, for a life carved from eternity.

With God, there's no "too late." With Him, should-be is still could-be. Your moment is any moment you say now.

"I run in the path of your commands,
for you have set my heart free.
... Direct me in the path of your commands,
for there I find delight.
Turn my heart toward your statutes
and not toward selfish gain.
Turn my eyes away from worthless things;
preserve my life according to your word."
—Psalm 119:32, 35-37

PART 2

ROYAL SINNER
A THRONE UNDONE

CHAPTER 4.5
UNDERNEATH THE
MORALITY-SUIT

"How the mighty have fallen!"

1 Samuel 27 — 2 Samuel 10

The King with One Eye Open

We've seen how God worked through an ordinary boy named David and how he became a great soldier and a future king.

We've talked about:

- Embracing self-worth
- Finding true strength in grace
- The power of friendship, and
- Knowing who-we-are.

David up to now has been a principled hero, and if we stopped here, we'd get the impression that the Bible is about glossy, photo-shopped, picture-perfect heroes. But if you know even a little bit about his story, you know the terrible things he's about to do that nearly undo him.

If the book of First Samuel was about David's rise to power, then the book of Second Samuel is his spectacular fall from grace.

I've always had a hard time with this part of the Bible because it's like watching a train-wreck in slow motion. It's worse because it's caused by someone I was rooting for. You know the part of the movie, when you're yelling at the good guy to choose the other door, to walk away, to put it down, to make the one phone call or say the one thing that will solve everything — but he doesn't, and he enters a disastrous, downward spiral of his own making.

It makes you cringe.

But I've been that person, too. If I were watching myself in the theater, I would've cringed just the same. There are times I've completely undone every good thing I had.

It's easy to hate David. But I understand him.

I'm just as capable of the evil he committed, if not more. And so are you.

—

We see the first cracks in David's character shortly after he spares Saul.

Out of fear and desperation, David joins the Philistines. If you don't recall, this is the people of Goliath, the giant that David had defeated to subdue the entire nation.

This is also the very first time that we see David's inner-monologue, as 1 Samuel 27:1 says:

"One of these days I will be destroyed by the hand of Saul. The best thing I can do is to escape to the land of the Philistines. Then Saul will give up searching for me anywhere in Israel, and I will slip out of his hand."

It's a significant literary bomb, because rarely do we see such thought-bubbles in Scripture. David's righteous actions have done all the speaking for him, but the first time he reacts out of cowardice, it starts in his head. He forgets who he is, which leads to his first big sin.

Shortly after David joins the Philistines, they attack the Israelites, and King Saul commits suicide on his sword. Jonathan, the son of the king and David's closest friend, is killed in battle. David hears the news and falls apart in grief. He knows that he's at least partially responsible, and in a wild fit of rage, David has the messenger killed on the spot. Against all that David had done to attain the throne by peace, he ends up doing what he wanted to avoid most: taking the kingdom by blood.

David unceremoniously becomes king over Israel for the next forty years.

And for forty years, the blood never stops spilling.

The problem was that many of the Israelites were still loyal to Saul and continued to defy David. I think I would, too. As far as they knew, David was a traitor and a Philistine. Imagine your country's most popular general had defeated the most wanted terrorist organization, then defected to that very group to fight their battles, inadvertently leading to the death of your country's president, and then returning home to become the president. This sort of scandal would be almost impossible to resolve in the public eye — and in such a barbaric culture, opposing political parties wouldn't just argue over blogs and microphones.

King David had to rule with one eye open.

Only a chapter ago, David had wisely avoided such an unstable cycle of violence by interrupting it with grace and waiting it out. But his hasty decision to join the Philistines sets off an escalating in-house war between the House of David and the House of Saul, with a back-and-forth bloodbath in streets and bedrooms, until three of David's sons were killed.

This part of the Bible is extremely gory and tragic, an awful retributive loop of *lex talionis,* with the constant dread that anyone, at any time, could be killed. It reads like a Mafia tale, a hit around the corner, death crouching in every frame.

It starts at a swimming pool.

At the first official pool party between the House of David and the House of Saul, soldiers from each side sit across from each other in silence until Abner, the former right-hand man of Saul, says, "Let's have a fight." Joab, the right-hand man of David, is all in. Twelve men from each side immediately get up and yank each other's hair and stab each other to death. Twenty-four men are laid out, knives wobbling in the air, blood blooming in the pool. The place becomes known as the Field of Hostile Daggers.

Joab's brother Asahel, of the House of David, chases Abner across a desert, and Abner begs him, "Stop chasing me!" Asahel keeps chasing, so Abner tilts up the bottom end of his spear to stop him. But Asahel is running so hard that the bottom of the spear impales him, bursting out his back.

Abner says the most sensible thing to prevent more escalation.

"Must the sword devour forever? Don't you realize that this will end in bitterness? How long before you order your men to stop pursuing their brothers?"

Abner strikes a deal with King David for protection, so David sends Abner away. But of course, Joab lures Abner to a public gate and stabs him in the stomach. Two of Saul's former men decide to join David and they kill Saul's son Ish-Bosheth by stabbing him in his sleep. King David then has the two men killed and hangs their bodies at the pool where it all started.

The House of David eventually wins over the House of Saul, but other nations are still attacking Israel. There's no moment of rest. David wages war against the Jebusites, the Ammonites, and inevitably, the Philistines.

If you haven't been able to follow what's happening, you only need to know: it's a mess.

Nearly everyone dies at the end.

To his credit, King David manages to stay above most of the carnage, standing back from the riptide of bloodshed and doing all he could to heal the kingdom. Though David indirectly bore so much tension by lapsing with the Philistines, he did his best to stay clean of the vortex and to re-right his people. He fought to lead. David publicly mourned and fasted for all of Saul's men and forced his own men to attend the funerals, and the "people took note and were pleased; indeed, everything the king did pleased them."[43] He honored Saul's son Mephibosheth, a disabled man, by having him sit at the king's table for dinner every day. David retrieved the sacred Ark of the Covenant, the ancient wooden chest that had the tablet of the Ten Commandments and the Torah scroll written by Moses, and re-established it as the center of worship. And as a judge and jury, the job of every king, David did "what was just and right for all his people."[44]

But you can see David testing the waters, slowly putting his feet into the stream of brutality. You can see when he begins to fake his outrage and mourning, when he lets his right-hand man Joab get away with every murder, when he uses his ex-wife as political capital. Just as much as the House of David and the House of Saul were at war, you can sense the war brewing in David, pulling him between his flesh and his divine calling.

Just as he begins to see light: the mighty David falls, and falls hard.

---

[43] 2 Samuel 3:36
[44] 2 Samuel 8:14

CHAPTER 5
A BRUTALLY HONEST, SURGICAL SELF-CONFRONTATION

"Why did you despise the word of the LORD
by doing what is evil in his eyes?"

2 Samuel 11-12

Someone Has to Tell You About That

A few years ago, I saw my friend wearing a bandage all the way around his upper-body from his hips to his shoulders. He looked pretty embarrassed. I told him, "You have to tell me why."

He said he got a call the night before from an old friend who was yelling, "Fight, fight at the beach, you got my back? Be there." My friend drove to the beach where there was a stand-off, but nothing was really happening. Someone pointed and made threats. Someone took off his shirt. Someone ran through the crowd, bumping into everyone. But that was it. My friend left.

On the drive home, my friend noticed his back was wet and reached under his shirt. A streetlight passed over and showed blood all over his hand. He turned to a hospital and checked into the emergency room.

A doctor examined him. My friend asked, "What's happening?"

The doctor told him, "Listen man, you've been stabbed."

Apparently, one of the guys from the other side of the stand-off had gotten a machete from his car and ran through the crowd and just went nuts. His hand became a piston. He even got a few on his side.

The doctor said, "Just another inch and you would've punctured a lung. Here's a bandage."

My friend finished his story and it was quiet for a while. And then I burst out laughing. I mean that kind of over-the-top, walrus-clapping, straight from the pit of my bowels kind of laughing. I fell over and nearly cried. I felt terrible, but I couldn't stop. My friend kept shaking his head, "You're sick, you're just sick." But he was laughing, too.

Can you really get stabbed without knowing it?

Later that day, the pastor side of me kicked in, and of course: I spiritualized the whole thing. I knew I was no different than my friend. There were plenty of times I had wounds that I didn't know about and I just kept living normally, even when it was obvious I was wounded. It took someone outside of me to say, *"Listen man, you've been stabbed. Here's a bandage."*

We live with these kinds of things all the time, these habits and excuses and grudges that never got the treatment they needed, and we wrap ourselves in lies until they're normalized.

You have a blind spot. If you don't think you have one, that's why they call it a blind spot.

And someone has to tell you about that.

All this has to be dragged into the light.

The lie has to be exposed, extracted, and obliterated.

One Awful Enterprise

THE DRAMATIS PERSONAE —

- King David, adulterer and murderer

- Bathsheba, the unfortunate woman taken by David

- Uriah, the husband of Bathsheba, loyal soldier and faithful servant

- Nathan, a prophet of God, bringing that truth-bomb

In the eleventh chapter of Second Samuel, we're told that David takes a break.

In the spring, at the time when kings go off to war, David sent Joab out with the king's men and the whole Israelite army. They destroyed the Ammonites and besieged Rabbah. **But David remained in Jerusalem.** (2 Samuel 11:1, bold emphasis mine)

This seems pretty harmless. David has been in battle since the first day of his reign, and he wants to sit this one out. Maybe he deserved a day off. No one would've blamed him for taking a vacation and queuing up his Netflix at home.

But David's break becomes a habit. In the next verse, we're told, "One evening, David got up from his bed" — which implies that a day off turned into a recurring pattern and David was sleeping until dinner time.

Let's pause here for a moment. In the first verse and a half, we learn two huge truths.

Every bad decision comes from 1) a bodily vulnerability, and 2) losing our urgency.

David was tired and he needed the rest. But when his tiredness dictated his routine, he was no longer in a state to make wise decisions. In such physical vulnerability, we're prone to let emotions drag us into dark rooms and strange places. We get a layer of fuzzy mold over our thinking. It might not be that your whole world is terrible: but maybe you haven't been eating right and sleeping well and you're in a bad mood. That's about the worst time to act in your own power.

David also let his guard down and let his urgency slip away, until his mission-driven life was replaced by luxury. Cruising by is our default setting. As Lecrae says, *"People do not drift toward growth and discipline. We tend to drift toward complacency."* [45] This is a much deeper issue than our physicality. Our energy has to be exerted somewhere, and if it's not for a bigger purpose, it either boils into *high drama over petty things* or *aimless living by lesser things*. I've been entangled in both. When I take my eyes off His glory for too long, I get spiritually out of shape.

---

[45] Lecrae Moore (@lecrae) Feb. 13th 2012, 11:30 am.
https://twitter.com/lecrae/status/169141389328785408

When we fall out of rhythm, we're more likely to get caught up in bad decisions. I don't say that to make you paranoid. It's not wrong to be tired or emotional or to take some time off, and we don't have to think about "purpose" every second of every day. But if we're aware of our own rhythms, we can be certain when it's not the best moment to decide something huge. It requires a self-awareness to know when your mind isn't at its sharpest. No one is expected to fully function one-hundred percent of the time, and it's okay to take a big step back until we've snapped back to ourselves. David could've slept all he wanted and rested as long as he needed, but his mistake was letting his state-of-mind take over his mind, so that his emotions became the engine instead of the fuel. And if what-we-do reinforces who-we-are, then David allowed himself to dwindle in a narrow funnel of laziness and lack of focus. His crash and burn was only a matter of time and temptation.

In the second verse of the chapter, David sees a woman bathing from his rooftop. It's possible that any other day, David would've grabbed his sword and crown and been on his way. But all his tiny choices have led him here. David sends for her.

One of David's men, thinking much more clearly, says, *"Isn't this Bathsheba, the daughter of Eliam and the wife of Uriah the Hittite?"* This is a reminder of the woman's humanity, but also that her husband was one of "David's Mighty Men," a champion of the army who had fought alongside David, "who gave him strong support in his kingdom, together with all Israel, to make him king."[46] Uriah had continuously risked his life in service of the king and his army. He had more than a passing knowledge of David; they had camped together during war, planned battle strategies, and celebrated victories.

David grabs Uriah's wife, sleeps with her, and sends her home.

These four verses of the Bible are told in such cold, unrelenting detail, with such a matter-of-fact tone, that any sort of legendary embellishment of David is impossible. And it gets worse.

Bathsheba gets pregnant, so David concocts a cover-up by getting Uriah drunk to sleep with his wife. But Uriah sleeps at the palace gate, declaring that he cannot go home in peace while his brothers are at war. He does this twice. David then sends Uriah to the front-line of battle so he could be killed.

As Tim Keller says, *"That's about half the Ten Commandments, being broken in one awful enterprise."* [47]

There are some sordid details that show David's malice and deceit. If Bathsheba had told David she was pregnant, it was most likely about two to three months before she knew, and then a week or two to send for Uriah, and another week or two until he returned. David's plan is just bad math. When he puts Uriah into battle, David secretly orders the men to withdraw at a crucial moment so that Uriah is exposed. Yet this also means that at least a few of Uriah's own men had to die in the front-line with him. And when the messenger brings the news to David, he

---

[46] 1 Chronicles 11:10, ESV
[47] Timothy Keller, "David and Bathsheba." Sermon preached at Redeemer Presbyterian. Aug. 23rd 2009

only says, *"Don't let this upset you; the sword devours one as well as another."*

By the end of the eleventh chapter, David has moved Bathsheba in to his palace.

We're told, *"But the thing David had done displeased the LORD."*

I would think so, too.

The Thing That No One Wants to Say

About a year has passed, and a prophet named Nathan drops in.

He tells a story about sheep.

"Hi, David. I need your advice on what to do. There was this rich guy who owned a ton of sheep and the sheep were busting out his barns and his farms and his cars, I mean sheep just everywhere. There was a poor guy who had one tiny little ewe lamb, and he raised her and bathed her and gave her food from the table and even let her sleep in his bed. So the rich guy drove by and took the poor guy's lamb and cooked her for dinner. What to do?"

We're told: *David burned with anger against the man and said to Nathan, "As surely as the LORD lives, the man who did this deserves to die! He must pay for that lamb four times over, because he did such a thing and had no pity."* [48] (12:5-6)

David has declared a death penalty for the rich man.

---

[48] 2 Samuel 12:5-6. I paraphrased Nathan's story, in case you didn't know.

Nathan replies, *"You. Are. That. Man."*

And then he goes off. Nathan says all the things that no one wants to say. He lists every evil thing that David had done and every good thing that God had given him.

> *"If all this had been too little, [the LORD] would have given you even more. Why did you despise the word of the LORD by doing what is evil in his eyes? You struck down Uriah the Hittite with the sword and took his wife to be your own. You killed him with the sword of the Ammonites."* (V. 8-9)

And he finishes by announcing a curse on the House of David, which would never find peace until the next king.

At this point, David could've said, "How dare you? Off with his head!" Or, "You don't understand, I was really stressed out." Or, "Nice story, I like you better than the jester." Or, "Yeah, I know I'm the man."

But David comes clean. *"I have sinned against the LORD."*

He unclenches his fist from his prison of lies.

David repents.

The Surgical, Sculpting Chisel of the Grace of God

"If someone can prove me wrong and show me my mistake in any thought or action, I shall gladly change. I seek the truth, which never harmed anyone: the harm is to persist in one's own self-deception and ignorance." [49]

— Marcus Aurelius

Why doesn't Nathan simply rebuke David on the spot? Why the long story and the strategic side-tackle?

It's because before confronting ourselves, we need to undo our **self-righteousness**.

We each have a nearly impenetrable fortress of resistance when we're called out on our wrongs. It keeps us blind to our blindness.

The way that God punches through David's self-deception is one of the most lauded turns of literary brilliance in written history. Nathan doesn't simply accuse David. In one of my old college textbooks, it says, "[Nathan's story] disarms David ... That is, it creates in him a sense of identification with the victim that outrages him and compels him to act. Only then is David prepared to reason objectively about what is good and what is evil and unwittingly stand in judgment of himself." [50]

In other words, Nathan peels back David's self-righteousness by turning his rules against him. David is knocked over by the

[49] Marcus Aurelius, 161-180 AD, *Meditations* (NY: Penguin, 2006) p. 50
[50] Darrell J. Fasching and Dell deChant, *Comparative Religious Ethics* (MA: Blackwell Publishing, 2001) p. 22-25

weight of his own standards. The very mechanism by which David has condemned the guilty to cover his guilt is finally turned on himself. His excuses have become his own liability, like a sword with a blade on both ends. It's what Jesus meant when he said, "For in the same way you judge others, you will be judged, and with the measure you use, it will be measured to you." [51]

David required a brutally honest confrontation, but it would take more than a lesson in theology or a list of sins. No one changes that way.

God rebukes David by first removing any possibility of an excuse or objection. God revokes David's self-righteous capacity to absolve his own sin.

David needed to confront himself, before the sight of God, without the slimmest avenue of escape or deflection.

If you want any hope of change, freedom, progress, recovery, and growth: you'll need to confront yourself, too. It'll be the most painful thing you've ever done, because we're so used to protecting our fragile, brittle egos. But it's more painful to stay stuck in the lie.

Our self-righteousness is a much bigger problem than we think. We'll do anything to filter out any evidence that something is wrong with us. There might be an overall sense that we're not "right," but self-righteousness is so entrenched in our guts that we'll bark and snap and weep and writhe our way out of responsibility for what's wrong inside. It's our most trained reflex.

---

[51] Matthew 7:2

If you've ever tried to confront your friend about their thing, you were amazed at their automatic defenses and sudden snarling. I'm sometimes surprised by my own excuses, too. When I'm guilty, I attack. It's the perfect way to get out of accountability. When someone does something wrong, it's all their fault, but when I do something wrong, it's my environment or my family or my stress. When we get caught red-handed, we go into a monologue of rehearsed responses that we almost really believe, because it took so many steps of rationalizations to get there.

You know what I mean. You have a friend who thinks they're passionate, but it's pride and anger. Someone is manipulative and they call it managerial. Someone is lazy and they call it "resting in Jesus." You have a thing, too. So do I. We live with the lie.

You and I experience this when the preacher goes off in the pulpit. "This sermon will be good for these people. I already do what the preacher's saying. I wish my friend were here to get this." I forget to look at the glaring, unwieldy plank in my own eye. We're constantly squirming to justify our own positions while condemning others for the very same reasons, because of our instinct for self-preservation. It's understandable; sometimes we're even right. The problem is, when unchecked, our righteous-radar throws everyone off the boat while neglecting to see when we're sinking.

When you want to escape by saying, "Well-what-about-them?" — God will twist you around to say, "Well-what-about-me?" The only thing that will destroy hypocrisy is humility. Part of humility is to quit holding up a mirror at others and to use it on myself first.

In God in the Dock, C.S. Lewis says that when we find Mr. X an impossibly stubborn person, we have to remember that you and I are also Mr. X to someone else. You and I have been the impossible person. "It is important to realise that there is some really fatal flaw in you: something which gives the others just the same feeling of despair which their flaws give you. And it is almost certainly something you don't know about ... But why, you ask, don't the others tell me? Believe me, they have tried to tell you over and over again, and you just couldn't 'take it.'" [52]

For the first time in a long time, David is being honest with himself before God. He lets the truth undress him. There's no place for him to run. His own judgment has betrayed him, and this is how God will work on us, too. He will dislocate your blame, one excuse at a time, until you really take a look at yourself and see you as you really are. Like Apostle James says:

"Anyone who listens to the Word but does not do what it says is like someone who looks at his face in a mirror and, after looking at himself, goes away and immediately forgets what he looks like. But the man who looks intently into the perfect law that gives freedom, and continues to do this, not forgetting what he has heard, but doing it—he will be blessed in what he does." [53]

We need help beyond ourselves. We need a Nathan. We need someone who can gently revoke our self-righteousness and apply truth to usurp our sinfulness.

---

[52] C.S. Lewis, *God in the Dock* (MI: Eerdmans, 1970) p. 154
[53] James 1:23-25

Here's how we see that grace is a surgical, sculpting chisel that renews us by confronting the worst in us with pinpoint precision and acknowledging our desperate need as sinners. Grace, after all, is a love that presses through sin. The God of the Bible doesn't merely drop a truth-bomb and beat you into submission, but gently removes your self-deception and empowers you to return home. It hurts like crazy. His grace does not merely comfort, but grabs your sin by the fistfuls and kills it with the relentless violence of love. It neither condemns nor condones, but convicts and re-creates. It's a scalpel that will work with you to the messy end.

It demands getting honest. It demands getting with those who will graciously rebuke you because they love you and know you can do better. It takes knowing that you might be wrong, that you might be blinded, that you don't have it right this time. It takes confession.

Honesty is the first step to healing. It's really difficult to confront your own ugliness inside. It's hard to confront your own selfishness; it's threatening to confess that you are wrong and sinful and flawed. But it's only with a reckless self-confrontation that you can be liberated from the lies you have believed. You can see the lie for what it really is. It's only by stepping back from the momentum of darkness that has swallowed up your vision that you will begin to see once more. The light is staggering, blinding, painful, and even humiliating, but to see yourself as you really are is to begin the path to be set free.

Our True Prophet:
Speaking Life Over Death

The root of the problem, of course, isn't self-righteousness.
A self-righteous bravado is only covering the real problem.

A rebuke might help for the moment: but for the long haul,
we need restoration to fix what's wrong inside.

Our deepest problem is sin. It's a spiritual disease of selfishness that causes us to hide from God and turn on one another.
And it's terminal.

Sin causes our self-righteousness, which then covers for our
sin. It's so tricky in that sin convinces us it doesn't exist, so that
not only does it break us, but we keep choosing it with our eyes
closed. Like St. Augustine said, we are *incurvatus in se,* curved
inward on ourselves, as a blade rolled backwards, a snake eating
its own tail.

After David is rebuked, he writes Psalm 51, a prayer of repentance. He says, *"For I know my transgressions, and my sin is always
before me. Against you, you only, have I sinned and done what is evil in your sight
... Surely I was sinful at birth, sinful from the time my mother conceived me."*

This points to an objective truth.

David has always been an adulterer and a murderer.

It was in David all along. His problem is your problem and
my problem.

It's him. It's you. It's me. It's sin.

David inadvertently gives us a clue about our condition when
he replies to Nathan's sheep-story. David yells about the thief,

"The man who did this deserves to die!" This sounds excessive; the only thing the Mosaic Law required for a stolen sheep was to pay back four-fold, which David correctly states from Exodus 22:1. Stealing sheep wasn't a capital offense. At first glance, the retribution of death is disproportionately outrageous.

Yet David's heightened outburst of morality isn't entirely wrong. Nathan probably drew out David's righteous anger on purpose. Robert Alter writes: *"Nathan may be counting on the possibility that the obverse side of guilty conscience in a man like David is the anxious desire to do the right thing."* [54] David has a *"compensatory zeal to be a champion of justice."* [55] He raises the standard to its inevitable, unbearable conclusion.

David has stumbled on an alarming truth: *that sin deserves death because it causes death just as much.*

Sin is always killing someone. The wages of sin are psychological, social, and spiritual death.

When we lie, it causes a distance between two people that erodes the relationship.

When we steal, it causes a void of resources that shrinks those who need them.

When we cheat, it causes a collapsed reliability that destroys the other person's peace.

---

[54] Robert Alter, *The David Story* (NY: W.W. Norton & Company, 1999) p. 257
[55] Ibid., p. 257

In the end, sin kills the sinner, too. It's an isolating self-absorption that deteriorates a human soul, and if he or she so chooses, will extend such breakdown into eternity.

Unless we kill sin, it will kill us: yet it's so much a part of us that if we killed it, we would be killed, too. *The death of sin is the death of you and me.* Like David, our own judgment of others would eventually come back to us. How do we fix us without being broken by the solution?

Most of the world tells us that the solution is to be wise, healthy, strong, kind, and generous. Every movie and song and book is spitting platitudes about a "victorious life," and the advice isn't all bad. But that doesn't even begin to make up for the trail of bodies we've left behind. No amount of advice or self-help or positivity is going to revive the things and people we killed. If you and I were to make a single slide of every crime we've ever committed and then project it on a wall in city hall, there's no good work that could wash away the stink of our sin.

In God Himself, we meet a glory so holy and perfect and flawless that we would be crushed by the depth of our own depravity. We don't have to do anything "wrong" to understand this, either. Even in the presence of human glory, around those who are smarter or more wealthy or attractive, we are pierced with insecurity and despair. Before a holy God: we cannot stand. There is no human righteousness that could keep us alive.

We need the gift of divine forgiveness, of a righteousness given to us by grace.

After David's confession, Nathan says, *"The LORD has taken away your sin. You are not going to die."* Nathan is confirming, "Yes, you deserve to die: but you won't." In order for God to be God, someone has to pay for justice to be wrought.

In a horrible judgment, Nathan brings the curse of sin upon David's kingdom and his entire household. David's first son with Bathsheba is struck with illness and dies, and later, David's own son Absalom turns against his father and does exactly what David did: covert murder and adultery by a rooftop. And when Absalom declares war against David but dies in the field, David makes the haunting cry, *"If only I had died instead of you — O Absalom, my son, my son!"* [56]

I'm not saying for a moment that when we sin, our children will pay. I'm not making that correlation. And I'm not saying that this isn't troubling, because God's sentence over David seems so harsh. Yet for one man, at this one time, the absolute penalty of sin was conferred upon someone else, in a way that I cannot fully understand, so that the man would live.

God is too holy to let us get away with sin, but He loves us too much to let us pay for it.

Years later, we're told of another child who had to pay for our crimes, too.

---

[56] 2 Samuel 18:33

In the life of one man who was the True King, we're told that God brought justice through a crucifixion.

And he was also a prophet, who declared over us, *"The LORD has taken away your sin. You are not going to die."* He was the prophet who took our death sentence upon himself, and even more, he declared, *"I am the resurrection and the life. He who believes in me will live, even though he dies; and whoever lives and believes in me will never die."* [57]

In a tomb, Jesus not only reversed death, but healed our disease of sin so that we would be renewed to a different kind of life. He has not only saved us from our sin, but saved us toward Him. The Christian is born again by the miracle and gift of His righteousness, so that we're no longer compensating for our shortcomings or running from our past, but fully confident in His Son, running towards His glory, free of shame and empowered by grace.

Before such a holy God, we're not only able to stand: but we are risen with Him.

It's never too late for this. You may feel impure, inadequate, haunted by a past, or living in the consequences of an irreversible choice. But God can restore in the wreckage there, so that what may have started off in a bad place can bloom to God's purposes.

David and Bathsheba began in the worst place possible and their consequences were severe, but they married and gave birth to Solomon, one of the wisest kings in Israelite history. I'm not saying that every evil deed has a silver lining, or that a deliberate

---

[57] John 11:25-26

disobedience will be delivered by God every time. I'm only saying that God is still there in the middle of your sin, extending the opportunity to turn it all around, and while you cannot go back on everything, you're never outside such grace that can finish your story well.

If you're there, my friend, in the middle of a bad choice that has already begun but has not yet led to implosion: I beg of you to repent, to back away, to find counsel, and find Christ again. As Apostle Paul said, it's God's kindness that leads us to repentance,[58] and God will hold off the consequences as long as He can, so that we may know we're better than the sin we've embraced, and that God has more for you.

"Create in me a pure heart, O God,
and renew a steadfast spirit within me."
— Psalm 51:10

A Word For You:
What Breaks My Heart Is When You Don't Hear Mine

Right now, you have a friend who needs a confrontation. Or you're the one who needs it.

I've always had trouble approaching someone with a fragile ego, because I know if I say anything disagreeable or honest, they'll defend themselves like crazy with a million excuses or

---

[58] Romans 2:4

throw insults or throw things off the desk or make ugly-cry-face and cut me off for a month.

I know this because it's me too. It's hard to hear the truth about yourself. Everyone knows the guy who *can't* handle rebuke — it's like walking on egg shells over thin ice over a minefield — and if you dare bring up a hint of contradiction, they will either melt down or throw things or suck you into a terrible black hole.

But without rebuke, we're left sauntering in an unseen cloud of darkness that threatens to destroy us by a gradual downhill fade. The most dangerous way to die is slowly, unaware, in descent.

A few years ago, one of my best friends was messing up with something. No one else knew but me. It probably wasn't a big deal, and no one would've been hurt if he continued, but I had to bring it up. I really didn't want to, but I couldn't just sit by.

My friend is the coolest guy in the world. I've never seen him rage out or say a harsh word in his life. He was the kind of guy who walked away from a group the second they began to gossip, who didn't hesitate to break up a street fight on his way home.

But even when I bring the truth to the coolest people: I've seen the worst come out of them. There's always a mirror-defense where they decide to bring up *your* grievances, or a lot of casual dismissal, or loud, angry hostility. Honestly, I was jaded to this sort of thing whenever I tried to confront someone, and I expected it to go bad as it always did.

On a Friday, we were hanging out at my place and I sat him down and started with the ominous statement, "I have to talk to you about something." My voice shook for that entire sentence. If I wasn't sitting down, my knees probably would've been shaking too.

I told him everything. I said, "I don't want anyone else to say something bad about you, that's why I'm saying this. You're my friend, you're my brother, I want the best for you."

After I was done, I braced myself. I physically reeled back, waiting for the shouting match.

My friend said, "Thank you" — and then he stood up without a word and went to the door, and he left.

For some reason, this was *worse*. I couldn't sleep that night. I thought I had totally screwed this up. Friendship, ruined. Years of loyalty, over. I kept going over what I said in my brain, all the ways I should've worded it differently.

The next day, my friend came by. He sat me down, the same place, the same chairs. He said, "I thought about what you said. And you're right. I'm going to stop immediately."

My entire body unclenched. To be truthful, I almost wept. I hate to cry in front of people, but I was just so dang relieved. Some of it was because I was emotionally tightened up, and some of it was my anxiety that I was no longer his friend. But mostly I couldn't believe that *another human being actually considered what I said and thought it was the best course of action, so he changed his life over it.* I was astonished.

It would've been okay if he cussed me out, or never spoke to me again, or kept living his life as before. I would've understood. I would've loved him the same. No one owes me anything, and this is not about him "following me." But the plot-twist is that he actually listened. Not to me, but to *wisdom*. I can't remember a time when it happened so quickly, so graciously.

He stuck to his word. He stopped. He went out of his way to make sure it never happened again. And I never tried to play around about it, I never said "I told you so" or "It's better now right" or "Aren't you glad you listened." If anything, we grew closer and stronger. I was one of the groomsmen for his wedding and he was a groomsman for mine.

Even in the best of friendships, rebuke is uncomfortable and icky and awkward, and if you ever get to that place of honesty, there will be a space of tension where the friendship hangs in the balance. There will be an initial emotional reaction. There will be dumb rationalizations and all sorts of frantic excuses and attacks. And I hope you can push past this. I hope you don't take it too personally. Every creature has an instinct of self-defense, and if you call me out, I will naturally fight back until I feel safe enough to open up. The only thing we can do is to endure the scratching and stumble through those first reactions, and maybe we can move past this part a little quicker each time.

I hope we can pursue rebuke, to pursue truth. I hope we are not overly sensitive to spiritual surgery. I hope you can run through my overreactions and get to that core inside, where you believe I can do better, and you sincerely do love me. I hope you will hear my heart breaking.

CHAPTER 6
THE RESTLESS BALLAD
OF A RUNDOWN WARRIOR

"My God, my God, why have you forsaken me?
Why are you so far from saving me,
so far from the words of my groaning?
O my God, I cry out by day, but you do not answer,
by night, and am not silent.
Yet you are enthroned as the Holy One;
you are the praise of Israel."

The Psalms

Full of Sound and Fury:
Signifying Everything

One of the most remarkable things about David was his doubt.

All through the Psalms, we see David contending with his doubts about God. Whenever there's a stanza of praise, it follows just as quickly with despair and confusion.

There are so many Psalms where David is singing in a flowery refrain of awe, but out of nowhere, he'll say, *"Do I not hate those who hate you, O LORD, and abhor those who rise up against you? I have nothing but hatred for them; I count them those who hate you, O LORD, and abhor those who rise up against you? I have nothing but hatred for them; I count them my enemies."*[59] It's all going so well, until you turn the page. These are like cysts that swell over the canvas, so jarring and troubling that you won't see them on coffee cups and Twitter.

David was really all over the place in his faith.

He wrote *imprecatory* prayers, which were angry, blood-soaked threats of vengeance against his enemies, and *lamenting* prayers, which were grief-stricken cries of misery.

These prayers are actually throughout the Bible, from the likes of Jeremiah and Isaiah and Naomi and Martha and Paul, when at one moment they praised God but the next they nearly cursed Him. The entire book of Nahum seems to be a racist, manic rant against the Ninevites, and the book of Habakkuk is a long fist-shaking session at God and the next door neighbors.

I've wondered:

Are we allowed to do this?

Are we *supposed* to do this?

I do believe that God wants for us to have a robust, thriving, fruitful sort of faith that trusts Him in every season. But at the same time, the Bible apparently has room for our screaming and shouting against the dark, and God can handle our very worst venting.

I don't think David is a template of who we're meant to be, but he's a reflection of how it really is: that we're often lost,

---

[59] Psalm 139:21-22

stuck, exhausted, even filled with hatred, and stretched between the abyss and the heavens.

I don't believe these doubts are momentary lapses of faith. I believe this is a *part of faith* — our fears, anxieties, uncertainty, and frustration — and it allows us to face the pain of our questions with honesty. You won't find this anywhere else, in any relationship or community or blogosphere. The second you doubt or disagree with your tribe, you'll be shot down or cut off, or at the very least, met with the stench of offendedness. If you tell your spouse, "I doubt you exist" or you tell your church, "I'm doubting your methods," or you tell the blog-world, "I'm doubting your protest," you'll be summarily analyzed or destroyed. It's only the honest dynamic of dialogue with God that you find true vulnerability, where you won't be vilified, but embraced.

The Bible also suggests that the journey of faith will have frequent peaks and valleys, with high points strung together by deserts and dry spells. In other words, doubt is unavoidable. We're sometimes taught in church that when we hit a rough season, to reach back for "how it used to be" on the mountaintop: but such self-imposed emotionalism only leaves us mired in guilt. We're not meant to duplicate the on-fire fervor of an old faith. The valley is the place where we're led to deepen our roots and pursue the reason to keep going.

I believe it's okay to doubt, and it has a direction.

"The waves of death swirled about me;
the torrents of destruction overwhelmed me.
The cords of the grave coiled around me;
the snares of death confronted me.
In my distress I called to the LORD;
I called out to my God.
From his temple he heard my voice;
my cry came to his ears."
— 2 Samuel 22:5-7

Stretched Between the Abyss and the Heavens

Just as much as David interrupts his own Psalms with rage and grief, these are rolled over by a sudden clarity of God's goodness, like a splash of cold water for bruised, bent hands. Most of the Psalms have a *Turn,* an about-face resolve where David recalls the truth about God's sovereignty. These upward Turns don't solve the situation, but they break David's fear and paralysis, and keep a terrible season of life from making him just as terrible.

In Psalm 13, the first truly disturbing passage by David, he writes:

"How long, O LORD? *Will you forget me forever?*
How long will you hide your face from me?
How long must I wrestle with my thoughts
and every day have sorrow in my heart?
How long will my enemy triumph over me?"

Then two verses later:

"But I trust in your unfailing love; my heart rejoices in your salvation.
I will sing to the LORD, for he has been good to me."

In the longest Psalm and chapter of the Bible, David writes in
Psalm 119:26 —

"It is time for you to act, O LORD;
your law is being broken."

David's anger against his enemies is palpable, but ten verses
later, he lands on mercy:

"Streams of tears flow from my eyes,
for your law is not obeyed."

These sharp Turns in the Psalms are a frail and feeble call to
remember God in the midst of so much distress. The deepest of
David was calling out to deep.

In David's prayer-life, we see both severe drops into depression and sudden bolts of euphoria, and we find a point of dizzy-
ing tension.

David managed to live with both complete joy and complete sorrow at the
same time.

He had a foot in the heavens and a toe in the abyss.

He had a frighteningly pessimistic view of the world in the
worst of his questions, but he was absolutely optimistic about a
God who was working all things together.

David let the gravity of his hopelessness sink in. The Psalms are full of yelling because David and the other psalmists don't hide under false coping mechanisms to dampen the pain. They hardly ever run to thrills and pills and religion and therapy, and if they do, they just as quickly run back. David allows the emptiness of his heart to take full course until the bottom gives out, so that he has no other choice but to find refuge in a bottomless God. The resolve of every Psalm could only come by scraping along the walls of a downward spiral, until there was a landing. It's in our full-on grief that we find the fullness of grace.

You might think, like I did, that David's sudden boosts of faith are a matter of "seeing God at work," that God always pulls through in some tangible way. And while great things happen to David, he also suffers dozens of lifetimes of pain. He has every reason to turn his back on God; unlike nearly every other person in the Bible, David never sees a single miracle. He never makes one, either. David's doubt could've been fueled by the absence of seeing the supernatural; he could've prayed for intervention at the level of Moses and Joshua, and it never came. But instead, David finds the simplest joy in God through the beauty around him, even as his own life tears at the seams. In Psalm 19, he writes:

> *"The heavens declare the glory of God;*
> *the skies proclaim the work of his hands.*
> *Day after day they pour forth speech;*
> *night after night they display knowledge.*

There is no speech or language
where their voice is not heard.
Their voice goes out into all the earth,
their words to the ends of the world."

David's optimism bursts forth by the simplicity of the stars puncturing the night, lighting up the earth and spinning in their quiet strength. They light up the Psalms in a woven thread of hope. David trusts in these foretastes of beauty, listening in to where God could be found, locking away these reminders for the next season of trial. For David, he couldn't rely on a splitting ocean or a miraculous healing or a resurrection. He finds God through the everyday, the almost mundane, things we take for granted, the seemingly random moments when dissonant notes fall in place and the chords catch his heart on fire. These rare flashes of the summit when holiness breaks in can't be forced. There's no formula, yet when they happen, they keep David alive in the valley because he sees God is truly real, and no one could take that away from him — not even himself.

It's this very trust in God, even when David sees no signs of Him, that is God's miracle being built, piece by agonizing piece. A person who sees little of God and still trusts Him is the *real deal*. As C.S. Lewis puts it so well, *"[Satan's] cause is never more in danger than when a human ... looks round upon a universe from which every trace of Him seems to have vanished, and asks why he has been forsaken, and still obeys."* [60]

You and I can do the same. It will look different for everyone. It could mean that you take a few days off, a long drive up, a place to volunteer, a place by the sea, hot coffee with a friend, a retreat of prayer, the wisdom of someone smarter, a fresh pen to a journal, a half hour with worship, a time to mourn and a time to do nothing. It might feel like going through the motions, but that's how recalibrating happens. You trace the sunbeam back to the sun, and you get a glimpse of our heavenly home, where He gives you the rest and resolve for your weary bones.

It won't erase the hurt or explain what's happening, but you'll get the pulse of a glory that keeps you alight in the dark.

"No man living beneath the copes of heaven dwells beyond the bounds of the diocese of God's Court-preachers; it is easy to escape from the light of ministers, who are as stars in the right hand of the Son of Man; but even then men, with a conscience yet unseared, will find a Nathan to accuse them, a Jonah to warn them, and an Elijah to threaten them in the silent stars of night. To gracious souls the voices of the heavens are more influential far, they feel the sweet influences of the Pleiades, and are drawn towards their Father God by the bright bands of Orion ... Even the sun shines in light borrowed from the Great Father of Lights." [61]

— Charles Haddon Spurgeon

---

[60] C.S. Lewis, *The Screwtape Letters* (NY: HarperCollins, 1942, 1966) p. 40
[61] Charles Spurgeon, *The Treasury of David, Volume 1* (MA: Hendrickson, 1876, 2011) p. 271

Our True Ballad:
We Cry Out, and So Does He

Many of David's prayers are prophecies that come alive a thousand years later in his own descendant, Jesus of Nazareth.

One of the most well-known prayers of David ends up being screamed from a cross.

Jesus, as he hangs bleeding, recites Psalm 22 —

"My God, my God, why have you forsaken me?" [62]

Everything else Jesus said in his whole life made sense, except this.

The *Cry of Dereliction,* as it's called, is a disturbing mystery. There are too many interpretations to count. Some say he lost the Father, or that he was identifying with us, or that this was a real cry of doubt. Some of these explanations are good, but they each come up short. And maybe that's part of the mystery. We don't really know why Jesus, the perfect Son of God, yelled such a thing.

We only know he did.

We cry out, and so does he. When I'm hurting, so is he. He both suffers with us, and for us, and "for the joy set before him endured the cross."[63]

---

[62] Matthew 27:46, Mark 15:34
[63] Hebrews 12:2

He was stretched with one hand in heaven and the other in the abyss, full of sorrow and full of joy, somehow both perfectly good and perfectly scarred, close to our pain and yet never overtaken. This is the safety where we can be honest, because no one was more honest than him.

This is a God I can worship. One who has sculpted galaxies, and has lived in one.

"I could never myself believe in God, if it were not for the cross ... In the real world of pain, how could one worship a God who was immune to it? ... I have turned instead to that lonely, twisted, tortured figure on the cross, nails through hands and feet, back lacerated, limbs wrenched, brow bleeding from thorn-pricks, mouth dry and intolerably thirsty, plunged in Godforsaken darkness. That is the God for me! He laid aside his immunity to pain. He entered our world of flesh and blood, tears and death. He suffered for us. Our sufferings become more manageable in the light of his. There is still a question mark against human suffering, but over it we boldly stamp another mark, the cross that symbolizes divine suffering." [64]

— John Stott

---

[64] John Stott, *The Cross of Christ* (IL: InterVarsity Press, 1986) p. 322

A Word For You:
You're a Preacher, and the Pulpit Is You

Right now, you have a song stuck in your head, and you might need to change the station.

One of my favorite Psalms is Psalm 42, sung by one of David's praise leaders, and probably written by David himself. The first four verses imply that David might have suffered from clinical depression and, at one point, had quit going to church for a long time.

"As the deer pants for streams of water,
so my soul pants for you, O God.
My soul thirsts for God, for the living God.
When can I go and meet with God?
My tears have been my food day and night,
while men say to me all day long, 'Where is your God?'
These things I remember as I pour out my soul:
how I used to go with the multitude,
leading the procession to the house of God,
with shouts of joy and thanksgiving
among the festive throng."

And then we find the Turn:

"Why are you downcast, O my soul?
Why so disturbed within me?

Put your hope in God, for I will yet praise him,
my Savior and my God."

This is really my favorite Turn in the whole Bible, because it shows exactly what we can do.

Here, the psalmist is *preaching to himself.*

The truth is that you have an inner-tape that plays all day long, just underneath the radar of conscious thought, but it's loud enough to control your world.[65] This tape is constructed from everything else you have ever heard about yourself, like toxins that have mixed into your batter.

Just as much as your life preaches a message to the world:

You're also preaching a message to yourself.

At some point, we must no longer be passive bystanders, but become an active voice.

Though David often doubted God, he didn't let this doubt run his life. At times he might have believed in a godless universe, but he never fully gave in to such a belief. When he slipped into his old habits, he completely repented and learned and clung to God's mission for His people. David essentially chose against himself. As best as he could, he counter-preached over his own feelings, and he acted upon that voice. It was this **self-defiance** and **God-reliance** that kept him grounded.

---

[65] I first heard this from Timothy Keller's sermon "Finding God." Sermon preached at Redeemer Presbyterian. April 21st, 2002

Dr. Martyn Lloyd-Jones, who wrestled with depression, wrote a famous insight on Psalm 42, which is a touch long, but without a wasted word.

"Have you realized that most of your unhappiness in life is due to the fact that you are listening to yourself instead of talking to yourself? Take those thoughts that come to you the moment you wake up in the morning. You have not originated them, but they start talking to you, they bring back the problems of yesterday, etc.

Somebody is talking. Who is talking? Your self is talking to you. Now this man's treatment was this; instead of allowing this self to talk to him, he starts talking to himself. 'Why art thou cast down, O my soul?' he asks. His soul had been depressing him, crushing him. So he stands up and says: 'Self, listen for a moment, I will speak to you.'

... You must turn on yourself, upbraid yourself, condemn yourself, exhort yourself, and say to yourself: 'Hope thou in God' — instead of muttering in this depressed, unhappy way. And then you must go on to remind yourself of God, Who God is, and what God is and what God has done, and what God has pledged Himself to do. Then having done that, end on this great note: defy yourself, and defy other people, and defy the devil and the whole world, and say with this man: 'I shall yet praise Him for the help of His countenance, who is also the health of my countenance and my God.'" [66]

And on Psalm 34, [67] he writes:

"After all, what we have in the Bible is Truth; it is not an emotional stimulus, it is not something primarily concerned to give us a joyful experience ... Truth is addressed to the mind, God's supreme gift to man; and it is as we apprehend and submit ourselves to the truth that the feelings follow." [68]

---

[66] Martyn Lloyd-Jones, *Spiritual Depression* (MI: Eerdmans, 1965, 2002) p. 20-21
[67] "Taste and see that the Lord is good."
[68] Ibid., 106

This is no simple cure and no easy task. It's work, each day, to simply preach the truth over yourself. Many of us are rehearsing a narrative of defeat over our lives, but we have such available grace to which we can cling again. It'll come down to the message that you're saturated in.

You are your own best preacher, and your pulpit is you.

Dear Christian: Preach to yourself. The Bible tells us multiple times to "recall" the truth to ourselves.[69] It's because we're forgetters. God knows this about us and He understands it. In a frantic moment or during a long season of pain, we enter a fog that dims the ultimate truth of our beloved status in Him.

Even if it's by a tiny shred of next-to-nothing faith, we can still recall, *I am loved.* It feels impossible, and even cheesy. But it's often just enough to get you through the next minute, the next hour, the next day. At the very bottom of ourselves, when there's no tangible help and no one else — we must be reminded of what we are. I am loved. As difficult as it is, it's no less true, and such truth can carry you through. You are so very loved, and His love is wholly complete.

Search me, O God, and know my heart;
test me and know my anxious thoughts.
See if there is any offensive way in me,
and lead me in the way everlasting.
— Psalm 139:23-24

---

[69] Lamentations 3, Isaiah 44, 2 Peter 1

CHAPTER 7
SO OUR SONG CLOSES,
THE FIRE RETURNS,
AND FAREWELL, MY FRIEND

"So be strong, show yourself a man,
and observe what the LORD *your God requires."*

2 Samuel 13-24; 1 Kings 1 and 2; 1 Chronicles 28

Unresolved Tension:
Holding On to Holding On

 I wish I could tell you that David's life gets better after his big, public repentance.

It doesn't. David continues to endure a web of misfortune and heartbreak. I would hate to end on such a downbeat note, but we find David in the last third of his life both scrambling for his legacy and frozen in apathy. We expect our heroes to have a happily-ever-after, but life is way harder than that. Reality closes in.

David's daughter Tamar is completely violated by her brother Amnon. Amnon is killed by another one of David's sons, Absalom. Absalom is banished and leads a revolt against his father.

David goes on the run again. Absalom is no match for David's men; he's killed in battle. David has now lost three of his sons and has essentially lost his daughter; he's cut short from grieving for them.

A civil war erupts between the northern and southern halves of the kingdom. Two of the leading rebels are killed to shut it down. But just as the north and south are re-united, a famine breaks out for three years, and the Gibeonite people demand that Saul's grandchildren be executed for atonement. David has seven of Saul's princes hanged.

Perhaps in a panicked zeal to keep the kingdom at peace, David takes a census for his army.[70] The census would've drafted men into the army against their will and taken illegal taxes from every soldier. It was also a narcissistic, self-measuring exercise of ego that would break God's law. Even Joab, the hot-headed, bloodthirsty pit bull of all of David's men, advises against it.

God doesn't let this one go: He gives David the choice of three more years of famine, three months of invasions, or three days of a plague. David chooses the plague, and seventy-thousand people die.

The last years of David are a frantic jumble. He spends over half a million dollars to clean his conscience at an offering. He prevents yet another son, Adonijah, from throwing a coup d'état. And nearing seventy years old, he develops a sickness that leaves

---

[70] The Bible says that both God and Satan incited David to take the census illegally (2 Samuel 24:1, 1 Chronicle 21:1). It's a troubling discrepancy and not so easily reconciled, but perhaps the simplest explanation is that God was exposing David's corrupt motives, and Satan only exacerbated David's methods.

him constantly cold and shivering. David is in constant need of a bedside nurse, frail and feeble, a former shadow of his shadow — and it's perhaps his failing health that drives him to compensate for his failures, when he was at the precarious edge of meeting a holy, fearsome God.

Until David's last breath, there's one problem after another: some his fault, and some not, and some resolved, but many are not.

He lives on edge, never fully at rest until the end.

Catching Up to Who I Never Was

David's final words on his deathbed might not be what we expect from a great, dying king. But considering all that he's been through, they're also the exact words we expect.

He tells his son Solomon,

"I am about to go the way of all the earth." In other words: *You'll be here, too. We all get here.* David exhorts Solomon to follow the Law of God so that he may prosper and succeed. He encourages the nation to finish the Temple that he was never able to build. But suddenly — David orders a hit on Joab and Shimei for their injustices. Joab was David's nephew and ever-faithful general, who had murdered a whole lot of people to retain power, and Shimei was a Benjamite who cursed out David and threw stones at him when he was on the run. Like a Mafioso godfather, David

whispers to his young son, *"Bring his gray head down to the grave in blood."*

I can understand why David's last words were so harsh, so desperate. They're tinged by the painful wish to have gotten things right the first time around. He's trying to make his last amends and to deal justice where evil went free. He's squeezing an entire life's worth of work in the illness of his last days, and so would I. David has a lifetime of unsettled debt, and it's here in his final days that he wants to finish well.

In David's final frenzy, I can see the grief underlining his words and wishes. They're like the reported last words of Leonardo da Vinci, *"I have offended God and mankind, by doing so little with my life."*

We find the same longing in each of us. His urge to both destroy evil and pay off his own sin was sincere. But David felt that in his last throes, he hadn't done enough.

The Missing Piece in Our Peace

"God does not give us overcoming life: He gives us life as we overcome. The strain is the strength. If there is no strain, there is no strength. Are you asking God to give you life and liberty and joy? He cannot, unless you will accept the strain." [71]

— Oswald Chambers

---

[71] Oswald Chambers, *My Utmost for His Highest* (OH: Barbour, 1935, 1963) p. 155

If I were to interview David on his deathbed, he might have said the same things that we all do. *"I missed it. I missed God's best. I missed the life I could've had."*

Or: *I wish I could've apologized. I wish I could've spoken up. I wish I had loved better, laughed more, enjoyed more, given more, worried less, hated less, didn't settle for less.*

The thing is, David was both right and wrong.

On one hand, David sensed that he fell short in his life, and he did. We *know* there's a kind of life we should live, and no one knows this more than a person near the end. We have life-sized regrets that will never be lived down, and if we each get the luxury of a deathbed, we'll inevitably mourn over the things we should've done. In fact, that points to the overarching truth of our condition. We're each held accountable to an unapproachable judgment that we cannot endure; we can't even withstand the judgment we place on ourselves.

On the other hand, David's over-fascination with getting it right was a hurried mess, and he beat himself up to the very end. Though he was responsible for most of his failures, there were too many elements out of his control. Even if he had done everything perfectly, the injustice of a sin-torn world would still have left him wounded. David had a burden to re-right every wrong, as we all should, but such a burden became a shackle of tightening sorrow.

A dying David realized two equally unsolvable problems: that the fallen world *outside* him was too cruel to fight, and the fallen world *inside* him was too crushing to bear.

He tried, in a sense, to crucify himself for his own sin and the sin of the world. He had seen so much ugliness, inside and out, that he longed for a peace he would never find.

You might think that David was awfully hard on himself, but we're not so different. The longer we live, the longer the trail of our own remorse. The older we get, the more we see our dreams are further from us, no matter how high we've climbed, because we're never quite the person we wanted to be, and we didn't treat others the way we wanted to. It's inevitable. It's nostalgia in reverse, a phantom of the universe we desired before it was replaced by the concrete curtain of reality. It's been famously called *Sehnsucht* or *saudade,* the "inconsolable longing" or the unnameable absence, or Jacques Lacan's inscrutable *Wunsch.*

We each have a picture of how we want things to be — but the sin of this world and the sin in our hearts will close in, and when reality settles, we remain disillusioned and unsatisfied.

There are times when it seems like nothing will get better. There are many times when it won't. Some of it is our fault, but much of it is not. We live on a fractured, fallen planet in which sin has coiled its tendrils through every movement and molecule, in which we'll be restlessly incomplete as we yearn for something "other." Sometimes things don't work out and we're left with the lifelong splinters of an insurmountable pain. There will be scars that we must live with until our time on earth is done.

We will lose some dreams on the way to eternity.

David had a dream for his kingdom. He had a dream for his children. He had a dream for his closest friends. He had one for himself.

But day by day, as he outlived his children and saw bloodshed take his friends and his nation, his dreams shrank and shook and shattered. David kept fighting, but life kept hitting back.

When he caught his breath, something else would happen and knock the wind out of him.

I've been there. You've been there.

Troubled sleep. A fog of muted panic. A knot in the stomach. The noose of self-condemnation. The constant dread that you're getting what you deserve. The fear that your friends might get hurt if they get too close. The haunting hologram of hindsight. Wishing to change those few seconds. Longing for the good old days. An apprehension of the future.

You've wondered if it's all for nothing. You've wondered if you can ever go back. You've had that Late-Night Regret Twitch, when you wish you hadn't said those words or moved to that city or gotten involved with that person or taken that job. You've heard sermons about "missing God's blessings" and how we can fall off God's Will and lose out on His plans. We scurry to achieve our best in our youth and feel at some point that *it's too late*, as if the ship has sailed and our best years are behind us.

All this sounds like terrible news, and it is. But confronting this knowledge is also the start to total freedom.

Kicking Off Our Shoes as We Kick The Bucket

Here's where I want to release you from something. It's something that I wrestle with, too, and I don't think I'm much further along than anyone else. But we need to be free of this. Ready?

You'll never fully obtain the idea of the life you've always wanted.

We will live with the phantom nostalgia as long as we live.

This is life. It's the inexorable spilling of sands through the hourglass as the door shuts on each day, the lights dimming to ash and embers.

It's hard. It hurts. It's itchy. There will always be something missing.

As C.S. Lewis said, *"Nothing is yet in its true form."* [72]

And this is part of living and dying, the part of being human.

Nothing in this world is truly going to meet the idea of what we always wanted. Every one of these romanticized ideas will eventually collapse in on themselves. They cannot make up for our mistakes or fulfill our eternal need. We'd have to constantly lower our expectations, which means settling for less, and that doesn't work, either. There's only one idea that will ever go so beyond our expectancy, that even our barest ideas of such fulfillment cannot compare.

---

[72] C.S. Lewis, *Till We Have Face: A Myth Retold* (FL: Harcourt, 1956, 1984) p. 305

He's the one we always missed even before we met Him. Underneath Him, we no longer need to keep unraveling, because He is the beauty that fills the crevices of an aching creation.

He is, as Lewis said, "the rumor" on the other side of the door, this imperceptible fullness that we now only see in glimpses of light through the slits of our human box.

The point isn't to lower our expectations. It's to raise our expectations so impossibly high that we know nothing will ever meet them: and then we discover The One who does, *for us.*

If we know a God who is the absolute satisfaction of our every passion, then He can release us from our discontent by the sheer nature of His perfection. He is our home: always warm and welcoming in our every condition, taking us in whether we've succeeded or failed, a place to recharge and gain resolve again, so that we can move into the world with a transcendent strength. We need such a home-base. Every one of us is confident in a place we can kick off our shoes and tend to our wounds. No matter what happens in the world, we have a Sabbath stronger than our circumstances.

Those who trust in God long for their true home, and already have one.

This doesn't mean, of course, that we don't try our very best. We're still meant to fight the good fight. We're still called to pierce the dark. David's burden on his deathbed was not wrong. But we're not beholden to get it right every time, and God doesn't really count the results. God's Will is less about what we do, but primarily about who we're becoming.

Even when we read of David now, we know he failed just as much as he succeeded: but it was his sincerity and authenticity that underlined his legacy. It's what separated him from Saul. It's the difference between Nicodemus and Caiaphas, or Naaman and Gehazi, or Jacob and Esau. It's what separated the equally stunning failures of Peter and Judas. They each messed it up, but God saw their hearts.

In fact, Solomon says of his father in 2 Chronicles 6, *"My father David had it in his heart to build a temple for the Name of the* LORD, *the God of Israel. But the* LORD *said to my father David, 'You did well to have it in your heart to build a temple for my Name. Nevertheless, you are not the one to build the temple."*

God saw that David had a dream that was pure and true — and though David couldn't follow through on building the temple, God says:

"You did well to have it in your heart."

It can be enough sometimes to try.

There's going to be a gap between our heart and our actions, always. But God counts the heart most of all, because when everything else is stripped away, this is what we bring to God at the edge of eternity. What matters is that we were the real thing, regardless of the results. And while we're fully accountable for where we've failed: God has us fully covered, if we so choose to embrace such grace.

The good news is that you're free of the life you've always chased, because God offers True Life no matter what kind of life you made for yourself. He offers Himself. God gives us both the grace to live today with everything we got, and a grace to assure us that we don't have to reimburse everything we missed.

You've probably heard something like this before and I know it's hard to wrap around this truth, but I hope we can get the immensity of God's heart for us. If you knew that your very best still somehow falls short, you could still do your best without the fear that it measures you or condemns you. Even more than that, *God gave you His best through His Son,* and we no longer have to weigh ourselves by our efforts, but His.

The life of Christ is the life we've always wanted, and needed.

If all this is true, and I believe it is, then the only permanent thing about your problem is that God walks with you right through it. Your very worst mess-ups are written in pencil, not pen. You can't "fall off God's Will," as if you could doom yourself to a mediocre Plan B, because God's Plan A is still His active grace. You can't "miss God's blessing," because the real blessing is that you're His. And you don't have to live in the fear of "unrealized potential," because it will be unrealized until our final glory.

We're in this gray space now, as 1 Corinthians 13 says, as seeing in an unclear mirror, and as 1 John 3 says, as beloved children who have not come home. Until then, some of your dreams on this earth will be crushed: but within the overarching grand narrative of God's rescue of humanity, you're free from the burden of living up to the false ideal.

Like David, you might have tried to be a good parent, a good leader, a good friend, a good spouse, and you failed all those things. You also looked for these things, but they failed you, too. It's only God through Christ who is the perfect father, leader, friend, and bride, who by His very presence can make us better at these things today, and will culminate our desire to have them in the end.

We're certainly called to deal justice and repent from our wrongs. We're called to spend our every waking moment with momentum: but the very reason we do those things is because we already have God, flexing in us, breaking in with His divinity to a world that needs Him.

We're certainly going to wade through the wreckage of some hard things: but none of it writes the ending on us. You won't write the ending on you, either. You have written in pencil. Only God writes with a pen.

"For David, after he had served the purpose of God
in his own generation, fell asleep,
and was laid among his fathers."
— Acts 13:36 (NASB)

"And what more shall I say? I do not have time to tell about Gideon, Barak, Samson, Jephthah, David, Samuel and the prophets, who through faith conquered kingdoms, administered justice, and gained what was promised; who shut the mouths of

lions, quenched the fury of the flames, and escaped the edge of the sword; whose weakness was turned to strength; and who became powerful in battle and routed foreign armies ... These were all commended for their faith, yet none of them received what had been promised. God had planned something better for us so that only together with us would they be made perfect."

— Hebrews 11:32-34, 39-40

"It can be so easy to think your whole life is in the moment, and that this moment will last forever, whether it is a beautiful or painful one. It is in these moments that we must either cherish them, or learn to live through them, because we will have other days filled with joy and pangs of sadness. This is life, like the changing of the tides and the rising and setting of the sun, things change and lives grow.

"You may be confused now, drifting away from what you thought would last forever; but know that you always have the choice to steer your ship back, that you don't always have to be left helpless in the sea of uncertainty. You have only to whisper, and in that action the winds will start to respond and the sails that once were useless will be the things that bring you home. You are not lost just because you don't know what the next step is, you are only in transition, it may be a long one, but it is only a chapter in an ever growing book." [73]

— T.B. LaBerge

"While other worldviews lead us to sit in the midst of life's joys, foreseeing the coming sorrows, Christianity empowers its people to sit in the midst of this world's sorrows, tasting the coming joy." [74]

— Timothy Keller

---

[73] http://tblaberge.tumblr.com/post/102746379926
[74] Timothy Keller, *Walking with God through Pain and Suffering* (NY: Penguin, 2013) p. 19

A Word For You:
Not There Yet

"But he said to me, 'My grace is sufficient for you,
for my power is made perfect in weakness.'
Therefore I will boast all the more gladly
about my weaknesses, so that Christ's power may rest on me."
— 2 Corinthians 12:9

Right now, you could be in the darkest season of this journey. You could be walking through the fragments of an old dream, and it will never be like it was before.

Our world is this muddy, middle part, where we're Not Yet Arrived but Now Fully Beloved. It's the world of the cross, where evil human hands crucified an innocent man, where God looks like He's lost control and that darkness has won the day.

But it's only for a day. Jesus has answered the pain of the world in himself. He tells us he is the true rest, the true refuge, our Sabbath, for the restless heart. He gathered the pieces of his disciples and his teachings and his miracles, and he breathed into them a new life, showing in one place at one time that not everything will end in a grave, but ascend to a home called eternity, where God has won. That's where we're heading, towards It is finished. It's where sin will be uncoiled, and we will finally be sainted and satisfied.

In Jesus, we have such a home.

We're not home yet, and that means nothing that happens here gets the final say on you. And it's because we're not there yet, we can do something now. Our time isn't waiting until the pain passes. Our time is meant to see bigger than the pain. We're on this mission, you and I, to bring healing into every corner of this fractured ground, to see His Kingdom flourish, to tell our story where our voice is needed: and to open our homes, to bring rest for the weary.

"And they admitted that they were aliens and strangers on earth.
People who say such things show that they are looking
for a country of their own.
Instead, they were longing for a better country —
a heavenly one.
Therefore God is not ashamed to be called their God,
for he has prepared a city for them."
— Hebrews 11:13-14, 16

FINALE
I AM DAVID

My name is David.

I was a king. I was a shepherd. I was the eighth son of Jesse, the fulfillment of an ancient prophecy for an everlasting throne.

I have seen many hard things in my time on earth.

I have seen arrows pierce the sunbeams over the Forests of Keilah, and the blood of my soldiers carried by the Jordan River in ribbons of crimson and gold. I remember the sound of a thousand chariots over the Desert of Ziph, the hooves of white horses upon sand and wilderness as the earth trembled, trumpets declaring all that we had won, louder than the enemies we had conquered. I remember the charred remains of my home in Ziklag, the fires burning across doorways and rooftops, when our wives and children were stolen, just as we had done to so many others. I have seen the end of many brave men, their eyes losing life, their armor too heavy as their swords fell before them.

I buried three of my sons.

I buried my only friend.

I married a woman whose husband I ordered to kill.

I have wrought many shameful sins in my seventy years.

It seems as a bad dream behind me.

Yet — I have seen many wonderful things. I have seen days of rain, my companions in battle laying down sword and spear to taste the fountain of heaven. I have seen the sun dipping below the horizon as the first stars emerged in a banner of purple, on the quiet hills of Mount Moriah. I have seen a nation torn apart, united into a kingdom. I remember my friend Jonathan, when he came to me in a field at the risk of certain death, and we prayed for one another, the last I ever saw of him as he called me his king.

I have beheld beauty. I have beheld such wonders of God, even in a world as ours, steeped in sin and sorrow, yet basking in a grace that I saw in a bare glimpse. I have seen light open up the dark and hold sway over evil.

I am here now, to behold the one above all beauty, from whence such beauty came.

I have seen many hard things — but our glory, such glory outweighs them all, and my heart has only begun to swell with new oceans of joy. The summit of our God is at once so high, yet so close, as I miss nothing, but there is ever more to see.

I have fulfilled my purpose, as much as a young child may please his father, with every effort so small and weak, yet every effort so loved and received.

I am here just a man in the stream of history, breathed into existence for a time, as but a torch shining briefly for God, for glory, for His people — for my Lord, who is to come as the Son of Man and bring you to Himself.

He is the King. He is the Shepherd.

May you meet Him, beloved, and live for Him.

I have known no greater honor in my time, and I will know nothing greater in eternity.

ACKNOWLEDGED

Thank you to every test-reader that invested your time and helped to shape this book to be better than I could have ever done on my own. You endured all those errors of verb agreement, my obsessive over-use of colons, and the artsy whimsy of "half-chapters." It's a scary thing to be so vulnerable with feedback, but each of you were both gentle and challenging.

Thank you to my wonderful wife; you listened to me read the book out loud and offered equal parts encouragement and fair criticism. I re-wrote two whole chapters for you.

I'm indebted to the expositions on King David from Jake English, James MacDonald, John MacArthur, Timothy Keller, Charles Spurgeon, and the Expositor's Bible Commentary, among many other great minds and resources. And I'm forever thankful for the great work of C.S. Lewis, who broke into my devout atheism over a decade ago and gave me the first hints of a coherent faith.

Made in the USA
Las Vegas, NV
02 April 2021